The Kookaburras' Song

John Alcock

The Kookaburras' Song
Exploring Animal Behavior in Australia

Illustrations by
Marilyn Hoff Stewart

The University of Arizona Press, Tucson

THE UNIVERSITY OF ARIZONA PRESS
Copyright © 1988
The Arizona Board of Regents
All Rights Reserved

This book was set in 11/13 Linotron 202 Berkeley Old Style Medium.
Manufactured in the U.S.A.

Library of Congress Cataloging-in-Publication Data

Alcock, John, 1942—
  The kookaburras' song.

   Bibliography: p.
   Includes index.
   1. Animal behavior—Australia.   2. Evolution.
3. Adaptation (Biology)   4. Zoology—Australia.
I. Title.
QL751.A585   1988   591.51'0994   88—4740
ISBN 0-8165-1050-4 (alk. paper)

British Library Cataloguing in Publication data are available.

To the National Parks of Australia and
the Australians who maintain them.

Contents

Acknowledgments

Many people have assisted in various ways in the preparation of this book. Dr. Alan Lill's invitation and financial aid from the Zoology Department at Monash University made it possible for me to go to Australia in 1978. While at Monash I received much useful advice about where to go and what to look for, especially from Andrew P. Smith and Graeme Suckling. My more recent sabbatical visit to Australia, referred to briefly in the book, was made possible primarily by Dr. Darryl Gwynne and the Zoology Department at the University of Western Australia.

Help in developing the illustrations for the book came from Bert and Babs Wells, John Cancalosi, Andrew P. Smith, and Promotions Australia through Terry Bransdon at the Australian Consulate-General in San Francisco. Marilyn Hoff Stewart did the original artwork with skill and enthusiasm.

Quotes used in the book came from Michael T. Ghiselin's *The Triumph of the Darwinian Method* (Berkeley: University of California Press, 1969) and *The Economy of Nature and the Evo-*

lution of Sex (Berkeley: University of California Press, 1974), Charles Darwin's *The Descent of Man and Selection in Relation to Sex* (New York: Appleton, 1871), George C. Williams's *Adaptation and Natural Selection* (Princeton, N.J.: Princeton University Press, 1966), and the *Reader's Digest Complete Book of Australian Birds* (Sydney: Reader's Digest Service Pty., 1976).

I am grateful to the University of Arizona Press for help in dealing with all phases of book publication. Kim Vivier improved the text with her suggestions, as did two anonymous reviewers. Many thanks to all of these, and to the biologists whose studies of Australian wildlife provided the foundation for this book.

The Kookaburras' Song

On Adaptation

Viewed from without, science appears to be a body of answers; from within, it is a way of asking questions. For this reason, the crudest approximation, if it provides hints for the solution of a broad range of problems, has every advantage over the most elegant mathematical law which asserts nothing of interest.

Michael T. Ghiselin

Darwin

NORTHERN
TERRITORY

QUEENSLAND

WESTERN
AUSTRALIA

Alice Springs

SOUTH
AUSTRALIA

Brisbane

NEW SOUTH
WALES

Perth

Sydney

VICTORIA
Melbourne

Australia

0   500   1000
Kilometers

TASMANIA

The Kookaburras' Song

The Australian aborigines supposedly believed that the kookaburras called the sun up from its bed each morning with their
hysterically noisy corroboree. I don't know how many of the
literally hundreds of aboriginal groups actually bought this
story. Perhaps it was even the fabrication of aboriginal infor-
mants eager to come up with something, anything to give a
visiting anthropologist something to record and reward. But the
myth possesses a ring of plausibility, and nonaboriginal Aussies
are pleased to repeat it. They claim that some aboriginal groups
enforced a taboo against joining in the dawn chorus of the
kookaburras on the grounds that this would interfere with the
awakening of the sun. After a winter's night spent out in the
open, blanketless, like many an aborigine in the history of Australia, I too would be in no mood to have anything delay
daybreak.

And it is true that kookaburras are specially prone to sing in
groups just as the sun puts in its first appearance of the day.

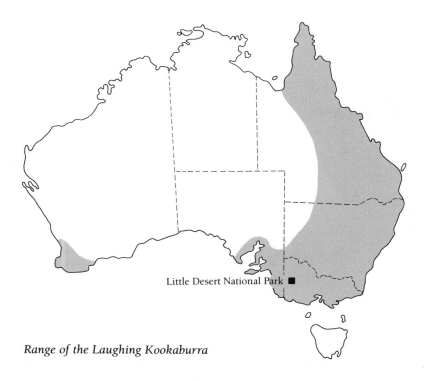

Little Desert National Park ■

Range of the Laughing Kookaburra

There is something about uninhibited communal laughter, especially if it has a crazed air about it, that infects the listener with a desire to hoot and holler too, and the first time we heard the kookaburras call the sun up, that is just what we did.

My family and I were camped in the Little Desert National Park, novices in Australia, unaware of the endemic taboos of the place, thrilled at having seen wild kangaroos the evening before when we drove up in our recently purchased but far from recently constructed Volkswagen campervan. I had bought the vehicle from a colleague at Monash University in Melbourne (where I was on sabbatical leave from the U.S.) despite warnings from other members of the Zoology Department that the campervan had been driven over unspeakable terrain during expeditions to the outback organized by its owner. Normally a cautious individual, particularly in the matter of car purchases, I must have been carried away by the exotic nature of my surroundings. Even though the van looked thoroughly exhausted, I found its history romantic and could hardly wait to settle in behind the wheel and head for some outback myself. The previous owner did nothing to discourage me in this ambition.

The trip to the Little Desert, several hundred miles to the northwest of greater Melbourne, was our shakedown cruise. In keeping with a near-universal policy of consigning to national parks those lands that lack or are thought at the time to lack any economic value, the officials in charge of the state of Victoria's park system called the Little Desert a national park after years of informal agricultural experiments had convinced everyone the place was worthless. How pleasant it is that some soils cannot grow wheat, for the Little Desert is a delightful scrubland filled with fascinating plants and animals. The surrounding countryside, however, affords wheat and cows an adequate living, with the result that in these places Australian biological diversity has been traded in for a numbing agricultural uniformity. This, no doubt, is how it has to be, but let us dwell on the positive and thank the luck of the draw that put lousy soils in a corner of northwestern Victoria and put us there, too, in a functional campervan. At least it was functional until I attempted to drive through a profoundly muddy stretch of dirt road in the park, thinking in my enthusiasm that the van would rise to the challenge in the confident manner of an experienced outback vehicle. Bogged to the axles and utterly immobile, my purchase began to lose its romantic aura rather sooner than it should have.

Nonetheless, we were substantially better off than Robert Burke and William Wills, two of Australia's pioneer explorers who were not rescued within an hour by a road crew with a Caterpillar tractor. Soon we were on our way again, albeit with a newly bent steering column, but not trapped in a real desert in the middle of Australia with death on the horizon.

There is a rich tradition of travel in Australia, from the early expeditions to the modern-day flood of tourists that journey, generally by plane, to the center of Australia in order to climb slowly up the rich red surface of Ayers Rock, usually in the company of several hundred of their fellow Aussies with any number of Yanks, Pommies, and other cosmopolites also in attendance. These travelers, pioneer and modern, have hoped to find something wonderful in a distant place, and who knows, maybe some have occasionally hit pay dirt. Most of the early explorers counted themselves lucky just to get back alive after enduring mile after mile of anonymous plains, dotted with porcupine grass and twisted little eucalyptus trees, or ridged with unending rows of sand dunes. Some wrote books about their experiences; others (including Burke and Wills) had books written about them—posthumously.

This book is a travel book, too. The scale of exploration, however, will be not transcontinental but biological, a trip to investigate what is worth wondering about in the lives of kookaburras and kangaroos. Mysteries abound in the behavior and evolution of the familiar animals of Australia. Although the geographical unknowns may have been neatly erased from this immense island, there is no shortage of things to look for and ideas to examine. The aborigines were on to something: the kookaburras' song deserves a myth, and the search for a modern equivalent of the aboriginal account has led me on a journey small in scale but large in pleasure.

We, too, can wonder why it is that kookaburras restrict their group concerts primarily to the early morning. The notion that anything so noisy and celebratory coming right at dawn must have some function associated with daybreak is far from unreasonable. The "dawn chorus" phenomenon is not limited to kookaburras but occurs in a host of other birds and some insects as well. Nonaboriginal biologists who have looked into this matter have asked, Why should the dawn singers voluntarily limit themselves to a few early morning hours of calling or chorusing? If there is a message in the kookaburras' hooting and laughter, why don't they propagate it at intervals throughout the day?

Two kookaburras, Australia's social kingfishers, one of whom has adopted the distinctive display posture of a calling bird.

Almost all modern biologists, myself included, are thoroughly grateful to Charles Darwin for having provided us with a way to gnaw on questions of this sort. The fundamental working hypothesis of Darwinian types is that whatever an animal does must be adaptive in the sense of helping individuals produce surviving offspring. After all, living members of an animal (or plant) species are descended from the most reproductively successful representatives of past generations, not from those that failed to reproduce. Therefore, individuals in the present should have inherited the adaptive capabilities that promoted reproductive success in the past. An animal's appearance, physiology, and behavior can be assumed to be perfectly adaptive, for the purpose of productive speculation, because less adaptive characteristics should have been replaced by superior ones as these arose by genetic mutation over the millennia.

Using the assumption of adaptation, the Darwinian's first job is to dream up an explanation for the way in which a characteristic, such as the dawn chorus of kookaburras, could increase the reproductive success of the singers. If singing at dawn were not the best aid to reproduction, why has it persisted to the present? Some of my imaginative colleagues in the scientific community at large have offered a possible explanation or two. For example, it may be that many birds and some insects sing at dawn because this is an unusually tranquil time of day. The absence of wind ripping through the vegetation is a big plus, if the goal of a singer is to project a message a long distance. Wind noise interferes with this goal, and since early morning hours are usually the least windy hours of the day, why not sing then instead of having to shout above the breezes later?

But there are other very different ideas completely in keeping with the Darwinian approach. The goal of a singer, particularly if he is a male, may be to attract a mate or repel rival males from his territory. If so, an individual might call and call for several hours at daybreak as a way of advertising what a terrific physical specimen he is, able to sing his lungs out on an empty stomach, going on and on thanks to his skill at having acquired plenty of food reserves on preceding days. By singing in the early morning before feeding that day, a bird forces his weaker rivals to do the same at a time of day when they are least able to fake being in good condition because of the night-long fast. Potential mates should prefer a male able to afford the costs of dawn song because such a male probably can offer more aid in parenting than a male in poor physical condition. Potential male competitors should avoid territory owners that can turn out honest advertisements of their endurance, for truly macho males in prime condition will be difficult to displace from their territories.

There are other ideas as well (perhaps birds sing at dawn because they cannot hunt as effectively then in the weak light of the early morning, so they broadcast their messages when it costs them less in the way of lost meals). All of which illustrates that Darwinians cannot rest on their laurels after coming up with a possible explanation for something curious. And they do not rest on their laurels. A speculation, a hypothesis, is only the first step in the search for the kind of evidence that will help toss out some possibilities while permitting one to be retained. We have not progressed very far with kookaburras per se for no one has assembled a complete list of competing ideas for the dawn chorus's function in this species and then set out to test the various hypotheses. But at least we know where to begin and roughly how to proceed. Just as the myths of aborigines probably gave structure and meaning to their interactions with nature, so too Darwinian theory and the assumption of adaptation provide a foundation for exploring animal behavior. We can listen to the kookaburras and hear intriguing questions in their mocking cries.

Selection and the Silver Gull

The kookaburras' song illustrates that evolutionary questions are far easier to devise than to answer, a fact that should not dismay us unduly inasmuch as a good question can be even more nourishing food for thought than a good (well-tested) conclusion. But although the high ratio of question to answer vis-à-vis kookaburra behavior is typical for the animal kingdom as a whole, some groups for one reason or another have been studied with unusual thoroughness. Thanks to Niko Tinbergen, behavioral biologist and Nobel laureate, gulls are one such group.

In the grassy campground at Wilson's Promontory National Park, an easy day trip from sullen, late-winter Melbourne, silver gulls and crimson rosella parrots have assembled on the lawn to beg for food from campers. We are there with our freshly repaired campervan. An adult rosella, its magnificent scarlet plumage patched here and there with baby-blue feathers, alights on my son's arm and finishes off chunks of cracker before moving on to nibble gently (luckily for Nick) at my offspring's ear, which after all looks rather like a cracker.

Range of the Silver Gull

Wilson's
Promontory
National Park

Rafts of waiting gulls regiment themselves on the ground, each bird equidistant from its several neighbors. Silver gulls are among the most beautiful of their group, with rich blood-red bill, legs and feet, pearly grey back, and immaculate white breast and head. Their brilliant yellow eyes survey us expectantly yet warily, rather like pickpockets in a fairground crowd. In the intervals between feedings, squabbles and fights break out occasionally in the congregation. Sometimes during these interactions individuals assume contorted poses, with neck stretched up to its limit and bill pointing down at an angle, or body held parallel to the ground but the head tilted uncomfortably upward, sharp red beak aimed at the sky. During these gymnastics the gulls utter strange cries.

Down on the park's great cove beaches set parenthetically between boulder-strewn points, huge overlapping petals of water, whose leading edges are thinly outlined in white foam, move slowly toward land, smoothing the fine brown sand again and again. At low tide in the evening, minute rivulets of water seeping from the upper tide line have cut a reticulated network of tiny channels in the beach. As the sun descends, there is a subdued aura of resignation in the still air, an uneasy feeling of Sunday's end.

No sounds come from the expanse of sand except for the splashing of scattered silver gulls. Along the water's edge a solitary gull runs in place, lifting first one crimson foot and then the other. As the gull paddles up and down it creates a small puddle that it examines reflectively. From time to time, the bird stoops to peck lightly at the water's surface before resuming its stationary race against nightfall.

The aesthetics of gull plumage, behavior, and habitat attracted Tinbergen to these birds in the first place and eventually led him to induce many Dutch and English students to join him in describing and analyzing the behavior of gull species around the world. In *The Herring Gull's World* (pp. xv–xvi) he writes, "Throughout the years of boyhood watching the life in the large gullery was complete happiness; and I derived a vague but intense satisfaction from just being with the gulls, feeling the sun on my skin, enjoying the scents of the lovely dune flowers, watching the snow-white birds soaring high up in the blue sky, and assuming, or rather knowing, that they were feeling as happy as I was."

When Tinbergen returned as an adult scientist to gull colonies to study their behavior, he brought with him an interest in the reproductive value of the traits he observed and an adaptationist perspective to make sense of what he saw. He and his colleagues concentrated on those components of gull behavior that can be catalogued as discrete communication signals, or displays. He labeled the "neck-stretched-up, bill-pointed-down" behavior the *upright display*, and gave the name *forward display* to the act of holding the body stiffly parallel to the ground. One of the key findings of Tinbergen's research group was that although there were subtle differences among the many species of gulls in the fine details of their displays, upright and forward displays nevertheless appear in recognizable form in almost all gulls around the world.

A cluster of animal species such as the family of gulls (Laridae) generally shares a set of biochemical, structural, physiological, *and* behavioral traits. This must be because they have inherited, from the distant common ancestor of all gulls, the genetic information that promotes the development of these shared features. Presumably the genetic basis for the first forward display spread through a now long-extinct population of protogulls from which all modern species are derived. As new species split off from the ancestral stock, they retained the key hereditary factors that survive today to shape the development of gulls' brains, which in turn regulate the repertoire of activities that a gull can perform. Thus the widespread distribution of upright and forward displays among living gulls can be explained as a by-product of the history of speciation that has occurred within the group ever since the founding species split into two.

Why have the genes underlying the development of upright and forward displays been retained in species after species of gull? To answer this question, consider why an individual gull employs a particular display. Niko Tinbergen observed that upright and forward displays generally occurred in tense, potentially aggressive situations, particularly when two individuals claimed the same important resource, such as a desirable food or a mating territory. He saw that the displays tended to follow or precede outright fighting when one gull attempted to peck at or escape from the other. Tinbergen felt that the displays conveyed to the rival the displaying gull's intent to engage in a physical fight. A bird with its head raised and drawn back in an upright display is in position to strike down with its sharp bill. Similarly, a silver gull in the forward display exaggerates the posture adopted by a gull charging to stab an opponent with its bill.

Tinbergen concluded that the origins of these displays lay in the conflicting motivations aroused by an aggressive interaction with a potentially dangerous rival. On the one hand, the bird is stimulated to attack by the presence of a competitor for food, territory, or a mate. On the other hand, the risk of injury induces fear or caution and a tendency to withdraw from the dangerous opponent. The result is an ambivalent behavior in which the gull adopts the posture of attack but does not actually carry

Two silver gulls employing the full forward display in an aggressive interaction.

out an assault on the other bird, at least not while engaged in the display. Over evolutionary time, so this argument goes, the displays of gulls (and many other animals) often become exaggerated and uniform across populations as a result of selection in favor of clear and unambiguous signals.

But this point begs a follow-up question: To whom are clear and unambiguous signals advantageous? What is the function of the stiffly executed forward display of a silver gull? One still-common view is that communication evolves to facilitate the spread of information and the resolution of conflict within a species so as to promote the survival of that species. According to this approach, no longer favored by most evolutionary biologists, a threat display is adaptive because it enables members of a species to settle their differences without fighting, thereby protecting social units against the disruptive effects of aggression and killing within the species.

The logical flaw in this approach becomes apparent when we perform a mental experiment in which the following conditions apply: (1) There are two types of silver gulls in a population, one that uses threat displays to benefit the species as a whole, and the other that ruthlessly assaults its opponents without prior attempts to use gentlemanly signaling to settle the argument. (2) The two types differ in their genetic makeup and therefore differ in the development of their nervous systems and aggressive behavioral tendencies.

The spread from one generation to the next of the genetic basis for "gentleman displays" versus "killer behavior" will depend *only* on the number of surviving offspring produced by the two types of individuals, *not* on the distant, future effects of these characteristics on the species' survival chances. If "killers" regularly leave more descendants than "gentlemen," gulls that employ threat displays will become rarer and rarer as time passes. The genetic basis for threat displays would eventually be lost from the species under these conditions—even though in the long run these genes might help the species as a whole.

Threat displays have not disappeared from populations of silver gulls and many other creatures. Therefore we can assume that in the past the ability to give these displays must have helped *individuals* to reproduce successfully. Any benefit to the species as a whole is incidental to the benefit to threat-displaying individuals as measured in terms of their ability to propagate their genes.

But what might these individual gains be? It could be that by having a battery of threat displays a gull is able to communicate clearly its motivation to defend or claim a disputed resource. The opponent receiving the message might conclude from an analysis of his rival's displays that the probability of bashing the displayer in an all-out fight is slight. If so, the competitor could gain by withdrawing before fighting, thereby saving time, energy, and a good bruising. The displaying bird also gains by not having to fight. Therefore, both signaler and receiver can, under some circumstances, benefit by resolving disputes at the level of threats. It becomes unnecessary to propose that "gentleman" fighters are actually sacrificing opportunities for personal gain in order to do good things for the species as a whole.

A study of the glaucous-winged gull, a relative of the silver gull, shows that these birds respond to threats in ways that clearly are in their own best interests. By placing stuffed models of gulls in existing territories and then manipulating the body posture of these dummies and their orientation to the territory holder, researchers were able to elicit very different reactions from the territorial birds. When the model was positioned in the upright display, it was more likely to be physically attacked by a resident than when it was in the forward display. This result confirmed Tinbergen's conclusion that the upright display signals a lower attack motivation than the forward display. If birds that give the upright display are more likely to flee than birds that are in the forward display, it is safer to attack them. The glaucous-winged gulls were less intimidated by opponents giving the upright display.

Even more revealing was the finding that when the models were placed at right angles to or were facing away from the resident, they were far more likely to be pecked than if they were turned by the experimenters (who controlled the models from a distant blind) to face the resident directly. A real-life intruder turning from a territory owner would generally be about to throw in the towel and leave. But rather than let the bird go in peace for the greater harmony of the entire species, the resident often takes advantage of the situation to sneak in a damaging blow or two, perhaps increasing the probability that the opposition will get lost and stay lost.

Thus, as expected from the perspective of individual benefit, gulls treat opponents that use intense threat displays with appropriate caution, for these individuals may be dangerous to them. But if they can jab a departing rival with little risk of retaliation they do so with alacrity.

Silver gulls and their relatives are not inherently sweet and gentle creatures, but they are not boring either, as Tinbergen knew very well. We can begin to make sense of their nastiness if we recognize that their behavior is much more likely to have been shaped by Darwinian individual selection rather than by some sort of "for-the-good-of-the-species" selection. This may be a bit disillusioning for the romantics among us, but somehow I don't think the gulls will mind if we view them with a certain amount of realistic skepticism.

Red-Tailed Black Cockatoos
Meet Dr. Pangloss

A long, lonely road far from Melbourne marks the southern boundary of Cape York, a vast and sparsely populated peninsula that juts into the Coral Sea like a huge finger directed at New Guinea. The road begins near the Atherton Tableland and wanders for hundreds of corrugated miles through an open grassy forest of dwarf eucalyptus, whose bent trunks and drooping foliage conjure up images of decay and degeneracy.

Late in the second day of traveling alone through what seems to be an eternity of emptiness, I encounter an improbable roadside stand in the forest. An outback farmer, neighborless in the wilderness, waits by the road to sell a bit of farm produce to the very occasional passerby. He discusses many things with me, commenting on the bird-watching ("Great fucking place for birds, none better"), cattle ranching ("Terrible fucking place for cattle, too bloody hot"), and old age ("Here, mate, why don't you give me a hand this weekend; I'm too old to do all the work this place needs"). I turn him down on the offer of employment but purchase a melon and, reacquainted with mankind, carry on down the endless dirt road.

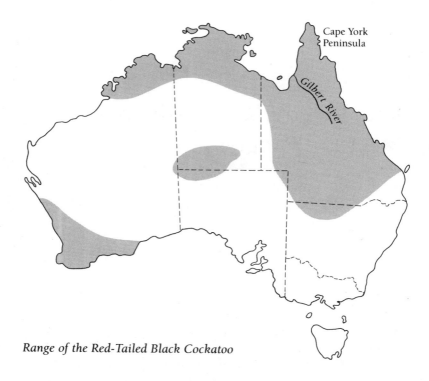

Cape York
Peninsula

Gilbert River

Range of the Red-Tailed Black Cockatoo

The bodies of dead wild pigs and kangaroos litter the road-side. They are killed in the night by huge road trains, powerful trucks that pull two or three full-sized trailers at speeds so great they seem to be flying over potholes and ridges. The beams of light from a tractor trailer's headlamps transfix animals as they cross the road or feed on the verge. They stare back blinded and confused for a moment. Most road trains in the interior sport massive, black, steel kangaroo catchers that leave behind a wake of carcasses for black kites, which perch with funereal solemnity in treetops along the highways.

The Gilbert River cuts north and west to empty into the Gulf of Carpentaria on the southwest edge of Cape York. The river is named after a nineteenth-century ornithologist, John Gilbert, who had the terminal bad luck to be speared to death by irate aborigines near the river on the first Leichhardt expedition. Natives accompanying the expedition had raped the wives of the spear throwers; Gilbert was unfortunate enough to get in the way when the aggrieved men came for their revenge. Ludwig Leichhardt survived this misfortune, but he did not outlive his last trip into the interior of Australia. There he disappeared without a ripple, but his name is appended to a river in northern Queensland and his strange life inspired Patrick White's novel *Voss*.

About halfway across Cape York the road slips onto a concrete ribbon of bridge only a few feet above the Gilbert River. In the middle of winter it is not much of a river, just a thin shallow band of water flowing erratically over a great sweep of riverine sands. On either side a lush green border of vegetation conceals the desolate forest plain beyond.

Agile wallabies occupy the strip, sometimes hopping into little clearings among the vines and eucalyptus where we can examine one another. A wallaby's eyes fill with anxiety and its body stiffens as it slowly comes to recognize me for what I am, the shape of an enemy. It then hurtles away in great kangaroo leaps straight through the entangling foliage.

On the river, plover pipe and scuttle on the water's edge while heron and ibis stroll in the shallows. A huge red-capped crane, the brolga, drifts overhead, occasionally flapping its pterodactyl wings while bugling a call that sounds as if it were produced by a combination wind instrument and plumber's invention. One egret chases another upstream; in its intent pursuit one white wing tip touches the black surface of the river, breaking the symmetry of its movements.

In the early evening red-tailed black cockatoos gather in trees along the riverbank and then launch out in twos and threes, gliding across pale sands to reach the dark line of water in the center of the riverbed. As the big black parrots come sailing in to join others already drinking at the water's edge, they wheel sedately in mid-air and fan their long tails to slow their descent; previously hidden deep red tail feathers glow for a moment in the tentative light of the day and then are extinguished as the birds settle on the sand.

I wonder about the purpose of those beautiful red panels in the tail of a red-tailed black cockatoo. Surely they have not evolved just for the appreciation of bird-watchers, but isn't it going a bit too far to try to read anything adaptive into them? And yet this is precisely what some biologists would try to do by asking what reproductive benefits might individual cockatoos enjoy as a result of their distinctive plumage. A traditional explanation is that the color pattern associated with a given bird species identifies an individual as a member of that species. Red-tailed black cockatoos differ from yellow-tailed black cockatoos in the manner you might expect, given their common names. Female red-tailed cockatoos might well use color pattern information to avoid mating with members of other cockatoo species and so gain by not producing defective hybrid offspring. Males therefore must carry their species-membership badge if they wish to be selected as a mate; only then will they have a chance to fertilize eggs, produce offspring, sow their genes in the next generation.

A nontraditional alternative explanation, however, is that the parrots read in the crimson patch of a flock member something about that individual's health and physiological well-being. It may be impossible for birds afflicted with parasites or illness to maintain the brilliance of carotenoid-laden feathers, and other birds may use this information to avoid their fellows with less than mint-condition feathers, particularly when selecting a mate.

This is the kind of adaptationist speculation that gets on the nerves of some critics of the approach, whose major spokesman has been Stephen Jay Gould of Harvard University. Gould has regularly flayed those who follow what he calls the "adaptationist programme" on the grounds that adaptationists "have become overzealous about the power and range of selection by trying to attribute every significant form and behavior to its

A red-tailed black cockatoo with its tail spread, revealing the red panels that give this parrot its common name.

direct action." Gould, who is not above using ridicule as a weapon in his attack, gets Voltaire and Kipling into the act by labeling adaptationists advocates of a Panglossian best-of-all-possible-worlds view of biology and inventors of fables as absurd as the fictional just-so stories of Kipling.

Gould and his allies note that although it is usually easy to dream up some hypothetical adaptive advantage for a trait of interest, the evolutionary process must often fail to produce the best of all possible characteristics. Selection has many constraints acting upon it, not the least of which are the erratically changing environments of many species over time. A current trait may be a holdover from the past, ill-matched to its present environment. Or an animal may be so locked into certain rules of development and anatomical interrelationships that it could not change these fundamental features even though a rede-signed animal would enjoy superior reproductive success. According to the Gouldian view, most animal and plant characteristics represent at best suboptimal, Rube-Goldbergian solutions to the problems an organism faces rather than perfectly adaptive answers to these problems.

The nonadaptationist argument has attracted much attention because of the forcefulness and skill with which it has been presented. This, however, has not protected it from the critical scrutiny of any number of Darwinists who have pointed out that Gould's Panglossian adaptationist does not exist in real life, at least if academic circles constitute real life. No biologist can succeed by coming up with one just-so story after another if he expects his ideas to be accepted on faith alone. Scientists insist on testing hypotheses, and the beauty of Darwinism is that it provides an adaptationist foundation from which it is possible to construct an immense array of testable speculations, stories, arguments, and ideas.

There is no question that some adaptationist hypotheses are silly, but as Jerram Brown has pointed out, these just-so stories are the kind that get discarded early in the game when the first test results come in. It would be unreasonable to expect every scientific hypothesis to be correct, and it would take all the fun out of science if this were the case.

For example, the idea that bright feathers are an adaptive signal of a bird's health and desirability as a mating partner was a highly speculative notion when first presented, and I am willing to bet that most biologists would have given good odds that the idea was dead wrong. But Marlene Zuk and William D. Hamilton tested their hypothesis anyway. They argued that if it was difficult to maintain brightly colored feathers in top shape under conditions of stress, birds with parasites would show diminished feather brightness. Going on, they claimed that if certain species were subject to heavy parasite pressure, healthy individuals of these species would have much to gain by honestly advertising their status through brilliant feather condition, for they would become more attractive mates. In contrast, members of relatively parasite-free species, having less to gain from such an advertisement, would be unlikely to evolve bright plumage because of its costliness to produce and conspicuousness to predators.

The stage was set for a testable prediction: bird species with colorful plumage would usually be afflicted with more internal parasites than those species outfitted with dull plumage. Zuk and Hamilton tested this prediction by taking data from the literature on the parasite loads of an appropriately diverse group of species. Then a person unfamiliar with the parasite data ranked the bird species from 1 to 6 on a scale of brightness of plumage. With these rankings in hand, it was possible to test for a correlation between plumage brightness and probability of parasite infestation. Bird species likely to be carrying blood parasites were also significantly more likely to have bright colors in their plumage than birds that for some reason did not usually have to deal with heavy parasite attack. By extension, it is not inconceivable (and it is testable) that red-tailed cockatoos use their tail feathers as honest signals of parasite loads.

The critical point, which strangely enough is not acknowledged by Gould, is that the adaptationist employs procedures that enable him or her to reject ill-founded explanations. The adaptationist does not sign a pledge to believe without question that all attributes of animals are adaptive; instead he uses the assumption of adaptation in order to test formally a particular argument about the possible adaptive value of a trait of interest. Zuk and Hamilton would have been badly advised to refrain from their adaptationist speculations on the grounds that they were running the risk of being overzealous (that is, wrong). They could find this out for themselves after testing, had the evidence refuted their predictions, and if so, no damage would have been done. No matter what the outcome of their tests, our understanding of the nature of bright plumage would have been advanced—by emphatically eliminating a possible adaptive explanation or by supporting it. It is no accident that most evolutionary biologists are Darwinian adaptationists who properly value a method that activates curiosity, identifies puzzles to solve, and offers the means to solve them.

New Holland Honeyeaters
and Adaptive Math

Toward the end of a month spent in Pearl Beach, a small resort town to the north of Sydney, I yield to increasingly plaintive requests that we spend at least one day in the big city. Momentarily suppressing my urbanophobia, I accompany my family to the megalopolis. We visit the zoo, Sydney harbor, the opera house, a revolving restaurant, and any number of shops along the way; we travel by train, by foot, by hovercraft, by bus— until it collides with a car, at which point we return to travel by foot, leaving behind a clogged street and the car's driver with blood trickling from a cut in her forehead.

Escaping from this disturbing big-city scene, we walk along a quiet tree-lined street in the older cobblestoned part of the port. On the way from one historical house to another I see my first red-whiskered bulbul. Usually I am pleased to be able to add a new species to my Total Life List begun in childhood. Here in Australia the listing instinct has been rejuvenated, given impetus by the stunning variety and novelty of Australian

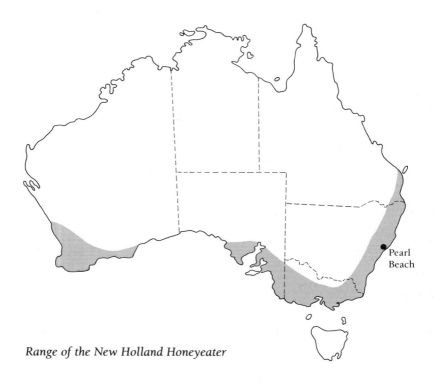

Range of the New Holland Honeyeater

birds. I have frayed my Slater's field guides, pawing through the pages to identify a new bird or in anticipation of what I might see in a new locale.

Having largely memorized the guides, I know at once that I'm looking at a red-whiskered bulbul when I see the sleek grey back, white belly, prominent crest, and red bars by the bill. There is nothing else like it. But the addition of the species, handsome though it is, to my Australian list gives me far less pleasure than checking off a new thornbill, despite the fact that thornbills are drab little birds, all of which look much alike. The red-whiskered bulbul is an escaped exotic; the Sydney population consists of descendants of caged birds released by or escaped from their human owners. Natives of China, they have no business in Australia.

Happily, they, like many other introduced birds, do not venture out in the countryside but live in the exotic urban habitats of their introducers. Around Monash I often see European blackbirds and Indian mynahs, released by persons in the past who were not content with one of the world's most delightful and wonderfully diverse avifaunas.

The same desire to be surrounded by the familiar led European immigrants to unleash European rabbits, European foxes, and European cats on Australia with disastrous results. Unlike the urban blackbird and bulbul, the rabbits, foxes, and cats have invaded all the continent, mowing down the native vegetation, gobbling up the native marsupials. Once while birdwatching in the Warrumbungle Mountains, I heard a sharp and disturbing scream come from a thicket of bracken fern (also introduced from Europe). The ferns parted for a moment as an immense orange cat fiercely pulled a rabbit to its death. Now exotic rabbits feed feral cats and foxes, helping maintain populations of these predators at high levels and enabling them to continue to depress populations of the far more interesting Australian animals.

Out-of-place rabbits and cats do so much damage that they give all other exotic animals a bad name, making it easy to feel a measure of disgust for all introduced animals everywhere. By altering the natural environment, they erase forever our chance to learn how plants and animals in an area have evolved together. Seeing the bulbul did not provide the kind of relief from city life that it might have. Instead it reminded me of who I am, an Australian immigrant, an exotic import, a member of a species so widespread that it lacks a distinctive native land of its own.

At Pearl Beach there are no bulbuls. Instead native birds, like the New Holland honeyeater, inhabit a coastal forest whose eucalypts, angophoras, banksias, and grevilleas are wonderfully new to a North American. "New Holland" is an archaic name for Australia, and how appropriate it is that it should be applied to a species of honeyeater, a family of birds indigenous to Australia and New Guinea. With their brush-tipped tongues, most honeyeaters make a living sipping sugary nectar, which is available at times in prodigious quantities from many Australian trees and shrubs.

A trailside banksia sports inflorescences of great complexity. Flower spikes as big as soft-drink cans rise from the tips of branches and stand stiffly erect, with a basal decoration of tough serrated leaves. Each spike contains a central woody core encircled by neatly ordered rows of hundreds of flowers with long thin styles. A pool of nectar lies at the base of each style, suggesting the plant's common name, Australian honeysuckle.

A New Holland honeyeater plunges its head into a banksia spike and drinks. When it withdraws its beak, its forehead is dusted with yellow pollen. Although it is gloriously patterned in black, white, and yellow, the eyes of the bird are its most impressive feature. They stare out of deep black cheek patches with a thoroughly maniacal intensity, black pupil within white iris. The Asian bulbul and European blackbird pale by comparison.

One bird spots another as it alights on the banksia. In a flash the nectar drinker darts from its flowerhead perch, chattering shrilly, and chases its fellow away. The two birds twist and turn acrobatically through the vegetation before the pursuer returns to reclaim its resource-rich shrub.

The New Holland honeyeater and most other members of its family have extreme sweet tooths. They survive largely on a pure carbohydrate diet of flower nectar from banksias, grevilleas, and eucalyptus, as well as the excreted carbohydrate covers (lerps) produced by small plant-sucking bugs (psyllids) and the crystallized sugar exudates (manna) from wounds in eucalyptus and wattle trees. The exceptional variety and abundance of these sugar sources in Australia may account for its remarkable numbers of honeyeaters. (Nectar, lerps, and manna were also exploited to good effect by Australian aborigines and white settlers. In the appropriate season a small group of workers could collect as much as fifty pounds of lerps in a single day.)

New Holland honeyeaters have apparently evolved such a

A New Holland honeyeater feeding at a banksia inflorescence.

strong reliance on sugar diets that they have a relatively reduced need for proteins, which are not present in nectars, lerps,
and manna. Honeyeaters occasionally hawk for insects as a protein supplement but only for an average of about ten minutes
each day, according to Australian ornithologist David Paton.
During a ten-minute bout a New Holland honeyeater can gather
only about 25 percent of the total protein thought necessary to
sustain a bird of its size. This suggests that the physiology of
the bird has been sharply modified by selection pressures associated with its specialized "junk food" diet.

Honeyeaters are not the only birds to rely almost exclusively
on a sugar-water diet. Hummingbirds in the Americas and sunbirds in Africa fill similar niches, and under certain conditions

some individuals in both groups will stake out and defend an exclusive feeding preserve. Several research teams have employed the "adaptationist programme" to develop testable hypotheses about food territories of hummers and sunbirds. These hypotheses have been based on the assumption that the birds are optimal economists capable of making decisions that maximize the difference between energy gained in nectar imbibed and energy spent in foraging and territorial defense.

For example, rufous hummingbirds in the western United States defend feeding sites during refueling stopovers on their long migration from Canada to Mexico in the fall. One group of researchers studying these birds was able to persuade territory owners to accept as a regular perch a modified precision scale that could be read at a distance with binoculars. This enabled the team to see how much weight the hummer put on as a result of owning a territory with a certain number of flowers on it. Individual hummers adjusted the size of their territories (and therefore the number of flowers defended) from day to day. The result was that the birds steadily improved their daily weight gain. In the space of four or five days a territorial hummer can gain fifty percent of its initial body weight to be stored as fat and used on the next leg of its demanding journey.

David Paton has examined whether New Holland honeyeaters also show adaptive flexibility in their territorial defense of food sources. He showed first that the number of honeyeaters and other nectar consumers in his study plot almost certainly could drink all the nectar being produced by the various plants during their flowering seasons. Therefore nectar was a limited resource worth defending. Paton watched his territorial honeyeaters during the fall and winter months, when the goal of the birds was presumably to get enough to eat to survive until spring, not to get fat for a migratory journey of the sort undertaken by some hummingbirds. He made the assumption that the honeyeaters were trying not to eat as much as possible each day but rather to get their minimum daily requirement of nectar as efficiently as possible so that much of the day could be spent resting safely in a sheltered spot away from the predatory eyes of local hawks.

If this was the birds' goal, the size of their territories should vary with the amount of nectar production in an area. When grevilleas were flowering, the birds guarded an exclusive domain only about twenty meters square, whereas when the banksia season arrived, territorial birds regularly repelled intruders from locations ten to one hundred times as large. Paton predicted that grevilleas must be a richer calorie source than the local species of banksia. To test this prediction, he measured the calorie production of individual flowers (which required him to enclose blooms in bags that kept the birds and insects away for twenty-four hours, after which he extracted the accumulated, unharvested nectar with a thin capillary tube and measured its sugar concentration in order to estimate its caloric content.) Once a value was in hand for calories produced per flower, it was a relatively simple matter to count the flowers in a bird's territory to come up with a number for the total calories available in the site. Paton then subtracted the calories drained off by insects, particularly honeybees, that are too small and numerous for honeyeaters to keep out.

When the mathematical dust had settled, Paton had a final figure of about eighteen kilocalories of energy available for the honeyeater owner of a twenty-meter-square patch of grevillea. This is just about what a bird the size of a New Holland honeyeater is supposed to need to stay alive and well for a day. As predicted, the banksias in Paton's study site generated far fewer calories per square meter, forcing the birds to defend much larger areas to get their minimum daily requirement of eighteen to twenty kilocalories.

If the function of territoriality is to enable a honeyeater to protect just what it needs to get by on a winter's day, increasing the number of calories available in an area should lead a bird to reduce the size of the plot it defends. Paton did the experiment by adding sugar water to flowers in a banksia patch. Sure enough, the territory owner contracted its preserve, reducing the amount of energy it expended in defense while securing its essential daily caloric requirements from a smaller patch of artificially "enriched" flowers.

Paton performed his observations and experiments in order

to test adaptationist predictions, and in so doing he demonstrated that New Holland honeyeaters are surprisingly sophisticated animals with the capacity to adjust their territorial behavior over a wide range of conditions. It is as if the birds had little calculators in their heads, whirring away all the time, adding up the calories required to defend an area of a certain size, plugging in data on the calories available in sugary nectar in potential territories, reaching mathematically complex decisions that enable them to defend areas of widely varying but appropriate size. Had Paton assumed that his birds could not possibly be smart enough to do these things, if he had not employed an adaptationist perspective, we would not know what fabulously adept mathematicians they really are.

Nuptial Puzzles

Hence we may conclude that it is the object of the male to induce the female to pair with him, and for this purpose he tries to excite or charm her in various ways; and this is the opinion of all those who have carefully studied the habits of living birds. But there remains a question which has an all-important bearing on sexual selection, namely, Does every male of the same species excite and attract the female equally? Or does she exert a choice, and prefer certain males?

Charles Darwin

The Unromantic Duet of Northern Logrunners

In Cairns on the north Queensland coast the tourist hustle gets going in earnest. The port is filled with boats, many of which will happily transport visitors on day trips to the Great Barrier Reef. Having fulfilled our duty in this respect we headed farther north to Daintree to look for crocodiles in the river there. We didn't see one but they were there, and some years later Daintree was the scene of a celebrated case of crocodile attack. The victim did not survive, and the unlucky crocodile lasted about a day longer before it was sent to its reward for having the temerity to feed upon a human splashing about in the Daintree River at night.

From Daintree the road north along the Pacific quickly deteriorated into a track suitable only for four-wheel-drive vehicles. I no longer looked upon our Volkswagen campervan as a valiant conqueror of muddy tracks, and it took no persuasion at all to turn the car west, heading for the Atherton Tableland, a plateau above the beaches. Here nestled somewhat incongruously amid ordinary farmland is Lake Barrine National Park, a

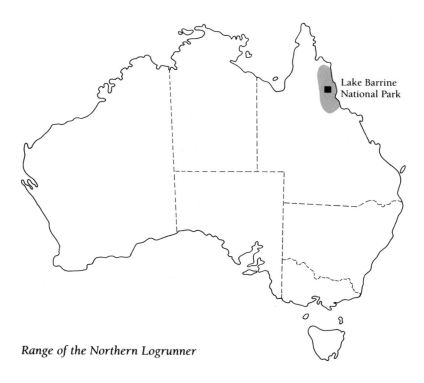

Range of the Northern Logrunner

tiny remnant of rainforest that encircles a small, clear volcanic lake. Tour buses bring the tourists that have had their fill of the Great Barrier Reef up to the lake in droves from Cairns. Most visitors briefly admire the view from a vantage point near the asphalted parking lot and then move briskly to the restaurant for tea and souvenirs.

On the muddy trail that circles the lake the roar of bus engines fades in the forest, which is largely composed of small saplings with white blotches and pink patches on their thin trunks. But scattered among the mass of ordinary specimens are enormous giants, buttressed and grey, that form an overwhelming canopy shading all things below. A riflebird clings to the trunk of one of the monsters, a kauri pine. The bird flakes great pieces of bark from the tree with its scimitar bill; the chips flutter down like oversized confetti.

Lianas hang in twisted lines from branches while spiny creeper palms spiral around the trunks of their supporting trees. Here and there a tiny shaft of sunlight penetrates the forest to illuminate a patch of damp moss on a fallen and decaying trunk or a bracket fungus, moist and yellow.

In the crumbling, sodden leaf mulch leeches wait patiently. When a hiker pauses for a moment, the spaghetti-thin, caterpillar-like terrestrial leeches urgently inchworm over the leaf mold, almost scampering toward their prey, if a legless animal can be said to scamper. When they reach a shoe they climb up to poke about for a place to attach their mouthparts. They are not fussy. A leech may choose to descend into the darkness of the shoe to find an opening in a sock through which it will insinuate its head or it may continue to ascend under a pant leg until it hits bare flesh. In either case, the leech will move quietly, avoiding detection, and it feeds with equal circumspection, slicing the skin gently until it opens a little wound where it will sup until bloated with blood.

It takes practice to regard a leech calmly, particularly when the creature hangs like a limp miniature sausage, fed to repletion, fat and blood-soaked, attached to an ankle, toe, or leg. Because leeches apply anticoagulants to the wounds they make, leech "bites" bleed for some time even after the bloodsucker drops off or is removed with exclamations of disgust.

Well above the horrid leeches, a boat-billed flycatcher perches like a yellow-and-black jewel on a limb, its flattened beak poised to snatch unwary insects from the air. Back on the ground, a northern logrunner sprints with Olympian speed along a recumbent moldering log stretched out across the forest floor. In body form and size the bird is reminiscent of a robin, although it has a black back, white belly, and vivid white eyerings. The logrunner stops abruptly to search for food, using first one large foot and then the other to push leaf litter to the side, looking rather as if it were doing a sedate conga. After a number of dance steps, it stops to snap up a victim uncovered during its maneuvers.

From among the dense and dark vegetation one logrunner begins to sing, a rich and powerfully resonant whistle that sounds as though it comes from a bird three times its size. The singer is almost immediately joined by another, and the two individuals, a male and a female, perform an eloquent duet that helps one forget for a time the hunting leeches.

Although uncommon among birds, duetting is not restricted to logrunners but is practiced by some South American flycatchers, African shrikes, and Australian and Asian babblers. The complexity of duet songs varies; the Australian whipbird, a babbler relative of the logrunner, exhibits a simple form. The male produces an extraordinarily loud and explosive call that sounds exactly like the crack of a bullwhip. This call is answered at once by the softer vocalization of the female. Some other babblers create far more complex duets that feature antiphonal singing, which requires each member of a pair to interdigitate a series of brief phrases, or song syllables, with a complementary series produced by the other bird. The composite song is so beautifully meshed that it sounds to a human observer as if it could only have been produced by one bird, not two.

But why is duetting adaptive for logrunners and whipbirds, but not for most other species? What is special about the environments of logrunners that has made the ability to sing a duet a reproductive plus for these birds? We can get at this question by taking advantage of the fact that there are any number of duetting species from many unrelated families of birds. Because duetting babblers, shrikes, and flycatchers do not share a recent common ancestor, each of these groups almost surely evolved duetting independently rather than inheriting it from a common ancestor. If it could be shown that unrelated duetting species share a similar environmental pressure pertinent to song communication, we could conclude that duetting is an adaptive response to this problem.

The British ornithologist W. H. Thorpe, who was one of the first to study duetting birds in detail, noted that these species usually live in dense tropical forest undergrowth or in other visually cluttered environments such as tall grasslands. This

rule of thumb applies to logrunners, which run about on subtropical forest floors, and whipbirds, which skulk in dense
vegetation on the borders of eucalyptus forests. Thorpe suggested that duetting could be a means by which a male and
female can maintain acoustical contact in an environment
where visual contact is easily lost. In this context, it makes
sense that duetting birds generally produce songs of exceptional loudness, the better to penetrate thick vegetation.

But what might the members of a pair gain by keeping in
touch, given the time and considerable effort that singing duets

*A pair of northern logrunners duetting on the forest floor at Lake Barrine
National Park.*

requires? As is usually the case with adaptationist arguments, several plausible alternative explanations exist. One is that the mutual calls substitute for the visual courtship displays that many birds employ as they get to know one another. A bird might be able to assess the physiological condition of a potential partner by judging how well this bird did in meeting frequent demands to sing precisely timed and very loud duets.

Logrunners and many other duetters, however, continue to warble together after courtship and pairing are over. Perhaps duetting can help the mated pair defend their valuable breeding territory. By calling as a duo, the pair gives clear notice to potential interlopers that two birds, and not just a single guard, stand ready to repel intruders. This may discourage invaders before they invade, saving the singing pair time and energy in territory defense.

There is, however, an alternative explanation for the evolution of duetting after pairing. In dense foliage a bird can easily lose track of what its mate is doing, and this creates risks of some significance. For example, an intruder male may slip into a territory and attempt, sometimes with success, to copulate on the sly with the resident female. If this happens, the territorial male may lose egg fertilization chances to his unseen rival, and so lose the opportunity to donate genes to the next generation. When male birds help rear the young of their partners, as the logrunner and whipbird do, a "cuckolded" male not only fails to fertilize as many eggs as he might have but also unknowingly helps perpetuate a rival's genes by assisting in the survival of progeny that are not his own.

Keeping an eye on a female partner during the time when her eggs can be fertilized has evolved independently in males of many species of birds that live in more or less open environments. Duetting may be an acoustical version of mate surveillance in an environment in which it is close to impossible to see what one's mate is doing all the time. By making continued assistance to a partner contingent upon joining in a duet on demand, a male decreases the chance that his mate will wander far from him and engage in an "adulterous" copulation with a neighboring male.

A study by Edith Sonnenschein and Heinz-Ulrich Reyer of duetting in an African shrike, the slate-colored boubou, confirms that these seemingly aesthetic ventures in cooperation have a more prosaic purpose. The shrikes apparently have one kind of duet in particular that seems highly likely to help the members of a pair keep tabs on each other. Males and females have sex-specific calls that serve both to defend a territory and to attract individuals of the opposite sex. A single male can, by giving his call, repel other males, for they will have to fight him if they come too close. The same call appeals to unattached females. Likewise, a female without a mate can defend an area against rival females while drawing in a new partner with her particular call. When a *mated* male or female vocalizes to defend a territory, he or she may also attract a member of the opposite sex. Needless to say, this does not sit well with the caller's current partner. The male's potential loss has already been described; a resident female could lose, too, if her male lured in a new female, for the newcomer might oust her from the territory or divert her mate from helping her and her offspring.

Therefore, Sonnenschein and Reyer proposed that the kind of duet that is composed of an alternating series of male and female mate-attraction calls has evolved because both individuals are trying to prevent solo-singing, which would bring sexual rivals flocking to the area. Thus when a male hears his mate signal, he quickly chimes in to announce to all the world that this female is already taken and newcomers need not apply. Similarly, when a female hears her mate sing, she immediately adds her note to warn other females that they will have to deal with her should they dare come closer.

If this interpretation is correct, certain kinds of avian duets may be the product of a conflict of interest between the sexes. A male boubou (or logrunner) has little to lose and potentially much to gain by inseminating a female other than his current mate, but his partner seeks to prevent this to protect herself. Likewise, a female that attracts a new male may secure a superior mate, or at least gain a certain amount of additional genetic diversity in the sperm of the interloper for the production of more diverse offspring. Her current partner, however, is the product of natural selection that has favored males able to thwart any tendency toward "promiscuity" on the part of their females. It is ironic, but instructive, to think that one of the most dramatic forms of harmony between individuals, a complex song duet, may be the result not of romantic cooperation between the singers but of underlying sexual conflict and competition.

Paternal Paragons
Among the Mallee Fowl

or A Dream (in Some Circles)
Come True

The ranger at Wyperfeld National Park tells me where to go to look for mallee fowl, a bird I very much wish to add to my list of Australian species seen and admired. I can pick up a short trail right to a nest mound, but the ranger warns me that the birds are diffident and my chances of more than a glimpse are slight at best.

A glimpse would be good enough for me, and I make for the trail, which slips into the mallee scrub forest, a uniform woodland in a land without topography. In the early morning the pendant leaves of the eucalypts filter the bright sunlight. Three galahs pass overhead, flashing in and out of view. The sun accents their parrot pinks while their thin calls fall to earth.

Each mallee eucalypt is a duplicate of all others, a fan of trunks only a few inches in diameter, spreading out and upward to a delicate crown of narrow, blade-shaped leaves that shade the forest from a height of ten to fifteen feet. The bark of the trees peels away from the trunk and dangles in curved strips that scrape in the wind before dropping to litter the barren ground.

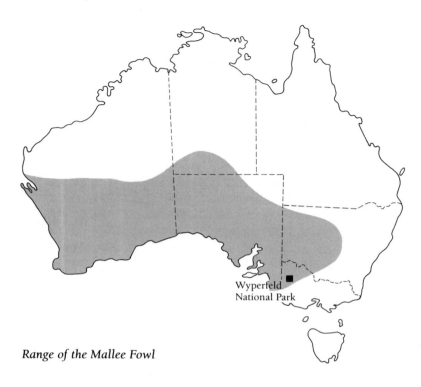

Range of the Mallee Fowl

I walk as quietly as possible through the absorbing woodland, stopping when I see a surprising mound, more than a yard
high and five yards across, which stands like a miniature volcano in a little clearing by the trail. Two mallee fowl stand
calmly in the pit of sand and forest humus they have excavated
within the center of the mound. They are beautiful birds, the
size of small turkeys, decked out in earth tones: greys, warm
browns, and off-whites. Their brown backs are scalloped into a
mosaic of large, leaf-shaped patches outlined in white.

I freeze as soon as I detect the mallee fowl, but as they show
not the slightest sign of alarm, I come closer. And closer. They
ignore me utterly as they face toward the center of the mound
and propel footfuls of debris out of the pit with powerful, raking leg strokes. Puffs of dust accompany each sweep of a leg,
enriching the metaphor of the mound as an active volcano.

Seeing how tame the birds are, I edge away slowly and then race back down the trail to the campervan, in which my camera has been left for safekeeping. By the time I return, the two birds have stopped excavating down into the mound and have begun to work at drawing material from the walls of the volcano into the center, refilling the pit they had constructed earlier. (I later learned that the mound is opened up in order to permit the female to lay an egg, which is then covered deeply with sand and debris.) But with the job less than half done the female walks up and out of the nest; she wanders slowly off over the hard-packed forest floor, stopping to peck here and there at cryptic food items.

The male remains behind, raking back five or six times in a row with one ponderous claw, then switching to the other for a new series of sweeps, moving from time to time along the rim of the now-diminishing volcano. The trill of a daytime cricket accompanies the methodical work of the mallee fowl.

After many minutes of exertion, the male completely reconstructs a smooth mound that conceals his partner's egg deep within. He stands on the top of the mound for a moment, then dips his head down, raising the plumes on his skull; while in this peculiar stance he lifts his wings slightly and utters a series of deep coos that roll off through the mallee forest after the departed female. I sit on the ground nearby and applaud his efforts.

K. H. Bennett, an early student of megapodes (mound-building birds, of which the mallee fowl is but one representative), appears to have been overwhelmed by the silent, claustrophobic mallee habitat and the tedious nature of the mallee fowl's routines. The *Reader's Digest Complete Book of Australian Birds* (p. 136) quotes Bennett as writing that the bird's "actions are suggestive of melancholy, for it has none of the liveliness that characterizes almost all other birds, but it stalks along in a solemn manner as if the dreary nature of its surroundings and its solitary life weighed heavily on its spirits." For an evolutionary biologist, however, mallee fowl are an absolute delight because their behavior poses many challenging questions. How did mound-building ever get started? What were the evolutionary steps that led from the typical nest-building behavior of most birds to the giant compost heaps built by mallee fowl and some other megapodes? And why do male megapodes perform most of the work of nest-building and incubation with essentially no help from their females, when females of most other bird species are full partners in these tasks?

The evolutionary sequence that led to meganests is not easily reconstructed, for there are no currently existing species whose nests seem obviously intermediate between a "typical" simple ground nest and the immense and complex nests of megapodes. But we do know that ground-nesting birds must contend with many egg-eating enemies, and one possible way for a parent to conceal eggs when it had to leave the nest unattended would be to cover them with forest litter. In tropical areas where leaf mulch is often moist, decaying mounds of debris would generate heat that could be used by incubating eggs. If a proto-megapode happened to bury its eggs deeply, the better to conceal them from predators, the eggs would also have been kept warm. What initially provided anti-predator benefits to a parent could provide incidental incubation benefits as well.

Almost all currently living species of megapodes inhabit wet tropical forests where they have access to quantities of moist organic material perfectly suited for making compost-heap nests. Therefore it seems likely that mallee fowl, the only megapode to inhabit cool, dry woodlands, have evolved from a tropical ancestor. Despite their spartan environment and a scarcity of compost starter that would lead an organic gardener to despair, male mallee fowl have successfully retained the ancestral pattern of using heat generated by fermenting vegetation to warm their mates' eggs.

It is the male, and the male alone, that devotes himself to the tasks of building a mound and tending the eggs after they have been deposited in his nest. Although a female may help a little in opening a prepared mound before laying an egg, the male does the rest. The job begins in the cool Australian fall, when the male laboriously digs a deep hole in the ground into which he rakes mallee leaves and other debris needed for heat production. He also gathers a great quantity of sandy soil to cover the composting center. This is a task that takes several months and a staggering amount of plain hard work. H. J. Frith, a megapode observer par excellence, discovered that males attend their mounds for about ten hours each day during all but one or two months of the year. Each day a male spends an average of more than five hours digging and digging, using his megafeet to open or build up the giant tumulus.

Eventually a male's nest is ready to receive the eggs of his mate; she lays them in the zone of the fermenting compost, one at a time at four-to-eight-day intervals. A single female may

A male mallee fowl working on his nest mound, which contains the eggs of his mate.

have thirty eggs to deposit over a period of several months. During all this time the male on his own, with no help from the female, carefully regulates the temperature of the eggs, keeping them to within a degree or two of thirty-three degrees centigrade. This task requires that the male measure the temperature of the material surrounding the eggs, which he does by taking up beakfuls of the stuff. If he determines that the fermenting compost has heated up too much, he opens the mound to let some heat escape. But when the compost has lost its warmth, the male may open the mound in midday to let the sun toast the eggs to a temperature optimal for development. Even so, two months of careful incubation are needed before an egg hatches and the fluffy youngster, fully active and independent, burrows up through the mound to set off in a dangerous world where it will be on its own from the moment it walks off the nest.

Once the compost-heap system of incubation had evolved, one way for a male to attract a female to him would be to demonstrate that he had a well-prepared heap of litter in which the eggs could be concealed and kept warm. Males of many bird species build display nests that show off the suitability of an area for nesting and the competence of the male to perform his parental duties. Females may use these display nests to make decisions about which male to select, thereby affecting the reproductive success of males. If the heat of the compost is sufficient to incubate the eggs in the female's absence, she could gain by abandoning the male with her egg(s) and devoting her time and energy to egg production rather than to incubation. Remember that a mallee fowl can lay thirty-plus eggs per year, a much greater number than produced by most birds.

A "deserted" male has two primary options: to abandon the eggs, in which case he will leave few or no descendants, or to care for them and attempt to attract his mate to return to the mound repeatedly to lay all her large clutch of eggs there, one by one. It seems obvious that the latter route is more conducive to genetic donations—provided the male inseminates the female whose eggs he cares for. Frith noted that males usually copulated before permitting their partner to lay an egg in their nest; without this precaution, their nest labor could be parasitized by males that undertook to fertilize females and leave the monumental job of egg care to the parental types in the population. The reproductive failure of those males would, however, shortly doom their genes and lead to the elimination of paternal behavior from the population. This has not happened. Instead, male mallee fowl work on, hour after hour, month after month, among the mallee eucalypts in an ordeal they accept stoically, unaware of the genetic dividend derived from their paternal sacrifices.

Cupboard Love and Thynnine Wasps

A mob of kangaroos flees through the woodland of black box eucalypts. They easily keep pace with the campervan as it rumbles along a dirt road in Wyperfeld National Park. Picking up speed, three roos race ahead and cut in front of the vehicle. Their great tails point to where they have been as they leap across the road and surge into a weedy field. A young joey not long out of the pouch is sandwiched between two adults. In great pogo bounds all three animals dash across the field and up and over a hill, advertisements for their special form of locomotion.

The black box forest forms a narrow band along a gentle depression that is irregularly flooded during periods of overflow from the distant Wimmera River. Floods of sufficient magnitude to reach Wyperfeld have occurred only three times this century, but these three have been sufficient to sustain the black boxes against invasion from the surrounding mallee eucalypts, which thrive in drier sandy soils.

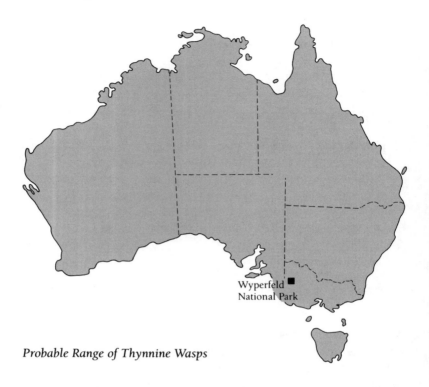

Probable Range of Thynnine Wasps

Scattered through the park is a necklace of lakes, each reservoir connected to the others by a thin channel. During exceptional floods they fill to a depth of six feet or so and then gradually evaporate, leaving behind memories of fishes and aquatic birds. In their place treeless pans form, ringed with eucalypt species whose seeds must be submerged completely to germinate. The river red gum grows to a great size with thick, twisted limbs. Branches break off as the gum outgrows and shades its lower limbs; the autotomized branches sometimes fall on campers attracted to the shelter of the tree, hence its nickname "widow-maker." Parrots nest in the cavities of the limb stubs.

It is the spring nesting season in a forest of river red gums, and I walk along with screaming cockatoos and galahs for companions. Their cries of alarm arouse distant birds and send eddies of noisy distress out from the trail. Four Major Mitchell's cockatoos flop heavily into a bare-branched wattle, their plumage a pale, greeting-card pink. They twist their heads from side to side, peering about in one-eyed agitation while flaring and lowering their beautiful salmon-colored crests in a semaphore of fear.

By the edge of the woodland, a little red-capped robin perches on a low stub and studies the grasses below with a flycatcher's concentration, oblivious to the raucous parrots. In scarlet, white, and black, it is as spectacular as the cockatoos, although its beauty is concentrated in a smaller package.

On a sand ridge above the floodplain forest, patches of porcupine grass stand at spiky attention, so sharp-needled that no mammal grazes here. Australian cypresses grow within some patches, which are their only refuge from the introduced rabbits that relish unprotected cypress seedlings.

Here on the sandy soil, some of the mallee eucalypts are in flower, their outer twigs adorned with blossoms, each a pale creamy white flare of thin petals surrounding a moist cup of nectar. Thynnine wasps dart from bloom to bloom, like hungry visitors at a food fair. Some of the wasps are copulating as they fly about, the winged males carrying the wingless females.

In one important respect male thynnines are like male mallee fowl, for they, too, offer a useful service to their mates in addition to providing sperm. By carrying his wingless partner to flowering trees and shrubs, a male wasp makes it much easier for his female to feed than if she were forced to crawl laboriously from one flower to the next.

Among the hundreds of species of thynnines, there is a fascinating variety of ways in which males help their mates. The males of some species merely transport their females *in copula* to flowers, and while the male drinks nectar from one blossom, his mate takes potluck at whatever flower she can reach. In other species the male's contribution to female welfare is more impressive, for he not only carries his mate about locked in copulation but also imbibes and then regurgitates nectar to her at regular intervals. Within this group are species whose males feed mates mouth-to-mouth and others in which a male carefully places a sweet droplet of regurgitate on a leaf so that the female may unravel from her tightly coiled carrying position to sip at his offering. In another somehow less aesthetic category are those males that drink nectar and then void an anal fluid that is avidly ingested by their females. All of these techniques have much the same functional consequence—by mating, a female gains easy access to food that she would otherwise have had to work hard to secure on her own.

It would be easy to interpret the helpfulness of male thynnines as their way of helping perpetuate their species, but by now we are wary of any such facile group-benefit explanation. Instead we must ask the same adaptationist question that we asked of the mallee fowl: What does a male wasp gain in terms of reproductive success by assisting his mate? It is clear what he loses. While gallivanting from flower to flower in the company of a current mate, a male cannot locate and copulate with other females, and so he loses some chances to fertilize eggs and pass on his genes. But this loss may be more than compensated for by other gains that we can identify once we understand something about the biology of female thynnine wasps.

Female thynnines are wingless almost certainly because wings interfere with efficient burrowing in moist, sandy soils that contain their prey, the larvae of scarab beetles. When a female finds a buried larva, she stings it and lays an egg upon the paralyzed victim. The egg hatches into a grub that consumes the much larger but defenseless beetle grub, and eventually the larva metamorphoses into an adult wasp that burrows up to the surface to reinitiate the cycle.

A newly adult female crawls up onto a grass stem or twig. Here she waits in a position characteristic of her species, often with her abdomen seductively elevated from the perch. In this pose, she releases a scent, a sex-attractant pheromone. The first male to fly to the end of the female's odor trail pounces upon his prize and carries her off. Copulation follows, and then a period of feeding while the two are still tightly linked. A mated

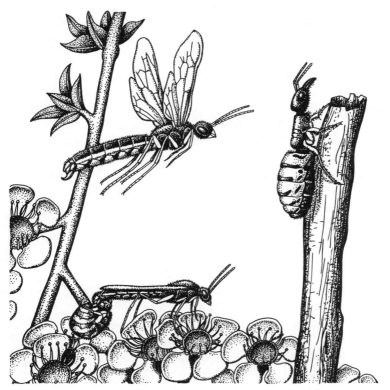

A male thynnine wasp flies toward a perched female that is releasing a sex pheromone. He will grasp and carry her away before mating. While copulating, the male carries his wingless mate with him and feeds her at intervals with regurgitated nectar.

female's abdomen gradually inflates with consumed nectar. After she is fully fed, the now-bloated female is carried by her partner to a likely spot for scarab hunting, their interlocking genitalia are uncoupled, the female falls plumply to the ground, and shortly afterward she burrows into the soil to start her search for prey.

Given the lifestyle of females, we can now imagine what might happen if a female were not given a hand by her mate.

We can be confident that burrowing through packed soil requires considerable energy. Without a partner's help she would have to find nectar on her own, and this would consume some time during which she might be captured or killed by a predator *or* found by another male, who might mate with her and supplant her first partner's sperm with his own. In either case, the original male's copulation would have netted him nothing, for he would produce no surviving offspring with this female. A male that feeds his partner reduces her solitary aboveground time, lowering the chance of predation and eliminating sperm displacement by remaining *in copula* with the female until she is ready to dig into the soil where she cannot be accosted by a rival male. The better fed she is, the longer she can afford to stay underground, the more beetles she will find, the more eggs she will lay, and the more of her mate's sperm she will use to fertilize those eggs. Therefore, males may actually produce more progeny by helping their wingless mates rather than by abandoning each female immediately after copulating in order to continue the search for still more mates.

This argument would be particularly persuasive if it could be documented that female thynnines fertilize their eggs with sperm of the last male to inseminate them prior to egg-laying (the phenomenon of *sperm precedence*). Although sperm precedence has not been examined in thynnines, it does occur in many insect groups and appears to be the typical result in species whose females mate more than once.

The advantages to males of helping would be further enhanced if females who were not sufficiently well fed retained their sexual receptivity. The nutritional condition of a female thynnine probably regulates her readiness to copulate. Individuals that have been digging underground for a time surface again and release a pheromone to call for a new male and a new meal. Moreover, if one experimentally separates a copulating pair prematurely, a simple matter of heartlessly pulling the two apart, the female (at least in a few species) will promptly adopt the species-specific mate-calling posture and attract another partner with whom she copulates.

This evidence makes more plausible the adaptationist argument that males help their mates only because females have made this the best way for a male to fertilize as many eggs as possible. It is almost as if males and females of one species are members of two distinct species, a conclusion that James Thurber appears to have reached in his *Battle of the Sexes*. The lives and goals of female thynnine wasps are obviously different from those of their males, a fact reflected in the dramatic sexual differences in their external appearance and behavior. The sexes may cooperate to some extent in the transfer of sperm and food, but only to further their separate reproductive interests and only because in some sense females have over evolutionary time been able to manipulate males to do helpful things for them. The nuptial gifts of males are offered in a businesslike exchange for eggs to fertilize because in the past males less inclined to make a deal were reproductive failures. The genes of these failures have disappeared, a lost footnote in a waspish history of sexual conflict and compromise.

Mate Choice by Female Hangingflies

Food Is the Best Aphrodisiac

The trilling of thousands of fat cicadas in the Warrumbungle Mountains fills the ironbark and white gum forest with a piercing summer song of painful intensity. We hold our hands over our ears and hurry down the trail, keeping a black-and-white willie wagtail on the run ahead of us. The little flycatcher has been hunting orange-and-brown butterflies that bask in sunspots on the path, and discarded wings of dismembered butterflies form a trail within a trail. The wagtail pauses on a stone, swaying from side to side, waving its large fantail as if reeling from the noise of the cicadas.

In a grassy forest clearing the chorus abates a bit. Burrow openings the size of a nickel lie scattered among the sparse grasses, with fresh mounds of dark soil marking each entrance. A huge digger wasp struggles over the ground, straddling the inert body of a big cicada that lies on its back, bright red eyes staring sightlessly to either side. The wasp forces its way to a nest, pausing for a moment before entering. It turns within the burrow to pull the silent cicada headfirst after it into its nest.

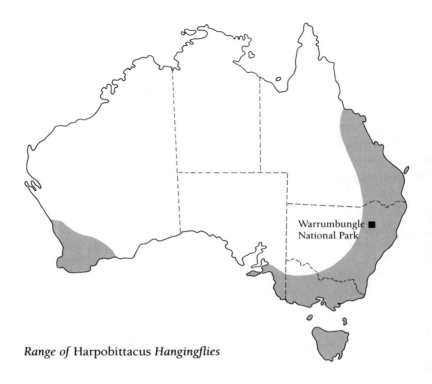

Range of Harpobittacus *Hangingflies*

The trail follows a creek downhill and eventually we escape the cicadas. A grey kangaroo watches with watery eyes from a tangle of shrubbery. The white trunks of the trailside scribbly bark eucalyptus are etched with meandering hieroglyphics carved long ago by larval insects.

In an open portion of the forest, where a hillside rises gently from the stream, a male hangingfly suspends itself from a little vine growing in a bush. It grips its perch with forelegs raised over its head so that it looks as if it is about to attempt a pullup. But instead it dangles freely, holding a dead moth with its hind legs. At regular intervals what look like two small bubbles inflate and poke out from between segments on the insect's lower abdomen. Currawongs call musically from the hilltop.

Hangingflies are not flies at all but belong to their own order, the Mecoptera. Like male thynnine wasps, males of many species within this group come up with nuptial presents for their mates. In place of regurgitated nectar, however, hanging-fly males offer something a little more meaty, a freshly captured insect for the pleasure of their predatory females. Males with a nuptial gift advertise the fact by releasing a pheromonal scent from the two inflatable dispensers on their backs.

A female that follows an odor plume will come to perch in front of her prospective mate. She grasps the prey gift and plunges her sharp mouthparts into it while the male urgently twists his long and flexible abdomen about in an attempt to couple with the female. If the seductive meal is large and nutritious, the female makes no effort to avoid copulation, the male retaining his hold on the perch while the female feeds for fifteen minutes or so. But if the male's offering is a very small insect or a nearly drained husk of a victim, the female after only briefly sampling the present will have nothing to do with the donor and instead flies off in search of a more generous partner.

Thus female hangingflies actively choose mates on the basis of the size and quality of their nuptial presents. This choosiness has obvious advantages for females, because the larger the nuptial present they receive, the less food they will have to collect on their own. Randy Thornhill has shown that hunting for prey can be dangerous because spiders wait on webs for searching hangingflies. A female filled to repletion with a nuptial meal can avoid blundering into a web while traveling through spider-infested underbrush; instead of foraging, she can spend her time laying her eggs, which she drops into leaf litter.

But why then do males accept the risky business of collecting food for their mates? The arguments developed for thynnine wasps apply with equal force here. By feeding his female, a male makes it possible for her to use his sperm immediately to fertilize the eggs she lays, rather than wandering about in search of food only to encounter a lethal spider or, and this is just as damaging from the male's perspective, another seductive male whose sperm will take precedence over his own when she fertilizes her eggs prior to laying them. Studies of a North American hangingfly strongly indicate that fully fed females become sexually unreceptive during the time they are laying eggs. But females of this species that have been offered an unsatisfyingly small meal go looking for another mate and copulate again before laying an egg. Female hangingflies make genetic success for males unlikely unless they assist them with an appropriately bountiful nuptial present.

The sophistication of female choice in these insects goes even further. Thornhill discovered that the number of sperm accepted by a female is proportional to the duration of copulation. By dissecting the sperm storage organs of females that were experimentally separated from their partners at various times during copulation and estimating the number of sperm contained within these organs, he found that when a pair had been coupled for five minutes or less, males had not transferred any sperm at all to their mates. Thereafter sperm were accepted at a steady rate for fifteen minutes, at which time the female had acquired a complete complement of male genes.

Under natural conditions, therefore, a male that cannot offer his mate a nuptial meal sufficient to entertain her for a full twenty minutes will fail to inject her with as many sperm as possible. Females that consume their gift entirely within twenty minutes terminate the copulation without ceremony and search for another partner whose sperm will dilute or supplant those they have just received. This makes it imperative that males not provide just any old nuptial present, but a hefty food gift if they are to fertilize as many eggs as possible.

Chivalry and generosity end, however, once twenty minutes have passed, because by then the male has transferred all the sperm he is going to donate. At this time he brusquely attempts to retrieve what is left of his nuptial meal, either for a snack of his own or to offer it to another female. His current partner often resists and an unseemly struggle results, with one or the other of the once-happy couple flying off with the prize.

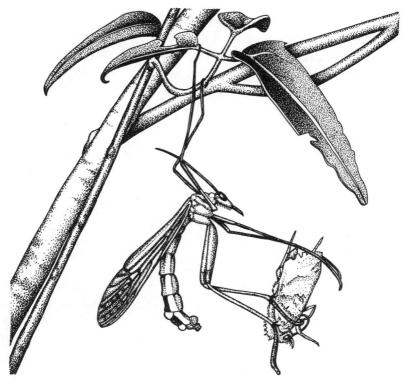

A male hangingfly with a nuptial gift, a dead moth, which he will offer to a female in exchange for a mating.

Thornhill has delved deeper still into the subtleties of female mate choice in studies of an Australian hangingfly closely related to the species that I watched in the Warrumbungles. Females of this mecopteran behave in the standard fashion of their group, rewarding males that offer them a large meal with a chance to fertilize some eggs. But females especially favor unusually large males and those that dish up an unusually large prey item. After coupling with individuals that exhibit either of these attributes, females tend to lay unusually large numbers of eggs before tracking down a new partner. They probably use more sperm from the favored males, granting them a relatively great number of descendants.

By fertilizing more eggs with sperm from the preferred classes of males, a female might produce more male and female offspring that will inherit the abilities that enabled their super-fathers to grow unusually large during their larval stages or to find and subdue large prey as adults. Either of these skills ought to improve the reproductive success of a choosy female, for either ability would tend to give her offspring a competitive edge in finding (or efficiently using) food in the larval or adult stages.

Through their materialistic choosiness, female hangingflies probably derive both more food resources for themselves and better genes for their offspring. The diversity and sophistication of their choice mechanisms, which operate to determine whether they will copulate at all, how many sperm they will accept from a given partner, and how many of a male's gametes they will use in fertilizing eggs, should encourage us never to underestimate the power of an insect's nervous system. A hangingfly's brain may be small in size, but it has been beautifully designed by natural selection to perform wonders of discrimination in the tricky nuptial maneuvers of these animals.

Machismo and
The Competitive Male

Inevitably there is a kind of evolutionary battle of the sexes. If a male attempts to reproduce at all in a certain breeding season, it is to his advantage to pretend to be highly fit whether he is or not. If a weak and unresourceful male successfully coaxes a female to mate with him he has lost nothing, and may have successfully reproduced. It will be to the female's advantage, however, to be able to tell the males that are really fit from those that merely pretend to be. In such a population genic selection will foster a skilled salesmanship among the males and an equally well-developed sales resistance among the females.

George C. Williams

Spotted Bowerbirds

Master Salesmen

Far west of the Warrumbungles, where mountains are just a memory, a sign by the Barrier Highway announces our arrival at another mountain range. But where the heck is it? We climb up a barely perceptible incline for a couple of miles and then descend with equal subtlety toward a sign on the other side of the "mountain." Only desperate eagerness for relief from the numbing uniformity of inland Australia could have inspired an explorer to make a mountain out of such a molehill in the Australian plain. North of the "mountain" the land flows smoothly without interruption from patches of prairie to stands of grey stunted trees and back again to grassland. Small eucalyptus trace the paths of the occasional watercourses. The land is close to featureless and it provokes a mild sense of uneasiness.

On a straight and unswerving dirt road we sail over the border between New South Wales and Queensland; our campsite is just off the road between Eulo and Cunnamulla. A feral pig charges from its hiding place and gallops wildly into the scrub forest as we drive into our bush camping spot.

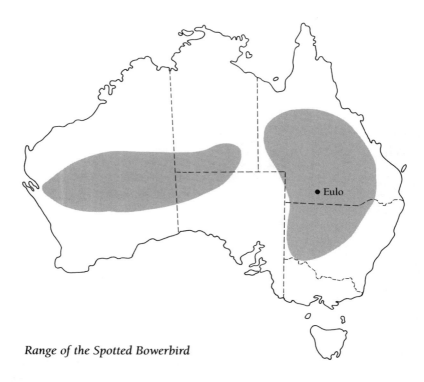

Range of the Spotted Bowerbird

In the late afternoon the red sandy earth glows again, no longer bleached by the sun. Noisy friar birds and spiny-cheeked honeyeaters call raucously before launching their brown bodies upward, snapping at the apogee of their near-vertical flights, and then diving back to the trees like spent but graceful rockets.

Plump black ants are crawling from dark nest tunnels to fly slowly up in the still air. They fly higher and higher as if determined to escape the evening shadows. But the friar birds and honeyeaters interrupt many an ascent with a sharp click of a beak. Those ants that survive the gauntlet will eventually mate, perhaps to found new colonies among the scattered patches of grass and trees.

A spotted bowerbird, chunkier and more earthbound than the honeyeaters, hops about, plucking ants with practiced nonchalance from the borders of their nest entrances and from tufts of grass. The grasses are dried and fragile, a paler brown than the plumage of the bowerbird, which runs confidently across the flat sandy sea of the outback.

Somewhere among the stubby trees near Eulo the bowers of spotted bowerbirds stand on the forest floor, looking like an outback child's creation. But the bowers are serious constructions, built by male bowerbirds as a centerpiece for their strange courtship displays. Males of some tropical species spend months assembling a huge mass of twigs, which they weave into fantastic roofed pavilions or twin towers that may be six feet high, depending on the species. They decorate the bowers with colorful flowers, fruits, lichens, or shells, creating a wonderfully playful effect.

Surprisingly, it was not until the 1950s that an Australian zoologist, A. J. (Jock) Marshall, showed conclusively that females took no part in bower building. Thus the fame of bowerbirds stems entirely from the prowess of males, and this seems appropriate in a country with a firmly established tradition of male chauvinism.

The bower of the spotted bowerbird is not so fantastic as some, but even so it is a clever piece of work. The bird stacks up and neatly interweaves dried twigs and grass stems to create two parallel walls about a foot high and a few inches apart, a simple but highly attractive and well-made structure. To further heighten the aesthetic appeal of the bower, the male paints the inner walls with a reddish-brown fluid composed of liquefied plant material and its own saliva. It also decorates the entrance of the avenue with bits of white bone, pale pebbles, and other whitish or greenish objects.

Males living near human habitations often collect bits of glass and aluminum to add to their display platforms, a common activity for several other bowerbird species as well that have an inordinate fondness for certain kinds of manmade trash. Satin bowerbirds, for example, go to great lengths to collect blue items for their bowers, and although they typically gather such things as the bright blue wing feathers of molting crimson rosella parrots, they are equally enamored of such throwaways as ballpoint-pen caps and fragments of blue plastic of any sort. In my one encounter with a bower-decorating satin bowerbird, the male came hopping toward his little avenue of twigs with a rubber band in his beak. It rather detracted from the naturalness of the moment despite the thrill of seeing a magnificent blue-black bowerbird at work.

Once a bower has been completed, a female may arrive to inspect it and its maker, and by all accounts this throws the male into a paroxysm of excitement. According to the *Australian Book of Birds*, male spotted bowerbirds generally respond to female visitors by running and bounding "rapidly in circles around the bower, while the female tries to hide behind the bower walls." A male may carry his enthusiasm to such a point that he literally trips over his own feet, a slip-up that can hardly be expected to impress his guest. All during these frantic maneuvers, the male sings, pouring out an astonishing repertoire that includes hisses, clicks, and mimicry of other birdsongs as well as of barking dogs and twanging fence wires.

One would think this would do the trick, but those patient ornithologists who have attempted to record the sexual behavior of bowerbirds all report that the vast majority of male-female encounters end in frustration for the male bird (and for the observer) with the departure of an indifferent female. Although copulations are few and far between, they obviously do occur occasionally, typically within the bower avenue or on the decorated bower platform. Apparently females make the rounds, dropping in at many bowers to have a look at the males' handiwork and histrionic courtship displays before finally picking a lucky male as a mate. Once a female is inseminated she can expect no help from her partner, who remains behind to tend his bower and to attract other females, while his mate deals with the more prosaic tasks of nesting and feeding the young entirely on her own.

The mating system of bowerbirds could hardly be more different than that of the mallee fowl. Why doesn't the bowerbird male put its energy into caring for its offspring with the same supreme devotion shown by mallee fowl males, instead of investing all in its self-promoting display platforms? How can a dedicated adaptationist claim with confidence that the extreme parentalism of male mallee fowl is a mechanism for the propagation of the male's genes, and then argue in the next breath that the male bowerbird's utterly nonpaternal behavior serves the same ultimate goal?

In order for males of both species to be acting in an adaptive fashion, the ecological pressures affecting bowerbirds and mallee fowl must be dramatically different, so much so that they

A male spotted bowerbird working on his bower, where he will display to visiting females.

have tipped the cost-benefit equation associated with paternal care in separate directions, leading to the complete "emancipation" of male bowerbirds from parenting. But what are the distinctive environmental factors that might have had this effect on the evolution of bowerbirds?

There are no complete answers to this question, in part because bowerbirds are tough animals to study and not many people have been brave enough to take up the challenge. But Richard Donaghey, then a student of Alan Lill's at Monash University, tackled the male emancipation problem. He took advantage of the fact that not all bowerbirds build bowers. The green catbird, named in honor of its catlike yowling, is one of the atypical bowerbirds; the males court females in a more traditional fashion by defending a territory in which the female nests. The species is monogamous, and although the male does not share incubation duties, he does help feed the nestlings.

Donaghey compared the behavior of the green catbird with that of the satin bowerbird, whose polygynous males mate with as many females as they can attract but fail to help any of them parentally. Donaghey found that only 25 percent of satin bowerbird females succeeded in rearing fledglings, whereas 65 percent of nesting catbirds produced at least one surviving offspring. Many of the failures experienced by the uniparental satin bowerbirds stemmed from nest predators. Female satin bowerbirds are exceptionally stealthy and cautious when approaching their nests, an indication that their nests are particularly vulnerable to certain predators that can detect inadvertent cues of activity at a nest site.

If it is generally true that satin bowerbirds and other polygynous bower-building species have especially potent nest predators, this would perhaps explain why females (and their mates) might not improve their reproductive success by having both parents, rather than just one, tending the nest. Visits may give away nest location to a lurking predator, leading to the death of the offspring.

There may well be other factors that have led to the evolution of nonparental male bowerbirds, but whatever the reason(s), males of most species do not currently assist their mates. Therefore a female's selection of a copulatory partner need have nothing to do with indicators of male parental skills. Instead, a female could, in theory at least, gain by choosing a mate whose visible characteristics somehow indicate that he possesses unusually "good genes," genes that will increase the survival and reproductive chances of the female's offspring.

The bowers and the male's frantic displays around them appear to be the evolutionary result of female preferences for males with extreme characteristics. In the simplest scenario for how this might come about, a female preference for a trait in the opposite sex can arise even by accident. Once the preference is established genetically, however, females will gain by mating with males with the preferred character because their sons will be attractive to the daughters of other females that have inherited the preference from their mothers. Males that happen to exhibit the trait in exaggerated form will be extra attractive, and the race is on for ever more extreme developments in twig manipulation, vocal displays, or bower decorations, each change spreading through the population and setting the stage for the next elaboration.

Some biologists feel more or less intuitively that the trait female bowerbirds prefer may not be purely random "aesthetic" characteristics, but rather indicators that do provide useful information about a male's heritable attributes. For example, female satin bowerbirds mate more often with males that have many blue feathers, snail shells, and yellow leaves beautifying the bower entrance. Gerald Borgia discovered this by setting up automatic cameras at many bowers; whenever a bird entered the bower avenue, it broke an invisible beam of infrared light coming from the camera and activated the filming mechanism. In this way Borgia caught 212 copulations on film and was able to identify the successful Don Juans in his population. The preferred males owned larger numbers of key bower decorations than the less attractive males.

The ornaments female bowerbirds find sexually arousing are all rare items, hard to come by, all the more so because male bowerbirds continually scour their woodlands for them. A male that is able to amass a superior collection of blue parrot feathers is a competent searcher, sound of mind and body. To the extent that his sperm contain genes that promote good searching ability, a female's offspring could benefit by receiving that male's genes. If the young inherit searching skill, they can use it in many profitable ways.

In addition, having a well-ornamented bower is indicative of more than just top-notch foraging skills. Males with numerous decorations tend to be strong, powerful, and vigilant, for they have to keep marauders away from their bowers, while they themselves stage raids to steal feathers and shells from the bowers of their neighbors. Male bowerbirds are notorious thieves and vandals, snatching decorations and demolishing someone else's meticulously constructed bower whenever possible. And why not, for the male that succeeds in destroying a rival's bower reduces that male's chance to impress a female, who may then come visiting his display site. Both Borgia and Donaghey have found that male satin bowerbirds spend most of their time close to their bowers, ready at a moment's notice to repel a stealthy intruder bent on undoing in a few minutes what the bower-builder spent weeks or even months to achieve.

Thus although male bowerbirds have enjoyed fame as a result of their endeavors as architects, artists, and actors, their behavior probably is primarily the evolutionary product of female sales resistance. The cold-eyed scrutiny of generations of females has left males chained to their bowers, like housewives to their ironing boards. There they must work to improve and guard their handiwork from ruthless competitors, and wait eagerly to produce on demand an elaborate courtship performance, only to watch female after female slide away to visit rival males. A difficult life, and perhaps one with a message for those persons afflicted with an excess of machismo.

Singing in the Rain

The Superb Lyrebird

Despite Melbourne's dedication to suburban sprawl and the supremacy of the automobile, there are places where animals live as they did before the metropolis existed. Sherbrooke Forest in the Dandedongs is a wonderful woodland on the eastern edge of the city, wild enough to make one forget the encircling highways and housing developments. Today the early hour and light drizzle make the park a place of damp darkness and winter solitude. Large black birds flop about in the crowns of a grove of mountain ashes, a monumental species of eucalyptus. Perhaps the birds are yellow-tailed black cockatoos, but there is too little light to say for sure. The mountain ashes shoot upward a hundred feet or more, pale trunks as straight and smooth as a fireman's pole except for scattered streamers of peeling bark.

My shoes squelch in the black forest muck; a small band of thornbills darns its way in and out of a tree canopy far above the mud and me.

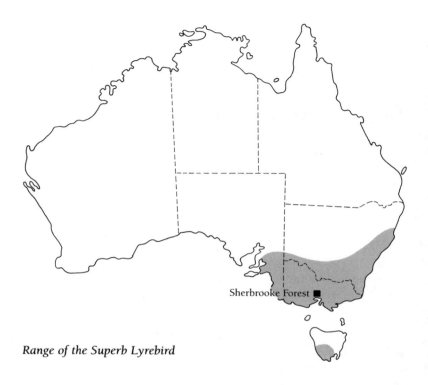

Range of the Superb Lyrebird

Nearby in a gully cut by a small brook, with banks of sodden undergrowth and palmlike tree ferns, a lyrebird's song knifes through the forest like a ray of light through a midnight room. The bird creates a masterpiece composed of a tumble of rich whistles, a medley of mimicked calls of whipbirds and cockatoos united with vibrant syllables of its own invention. The song builds to an almost painful intensity, ceases abruptly, and then begins anew.

The singing male stands on the moist trunk of a small understory tree that has been bent almost parallel to the ground. At first glance, the bird resembles a large chicken with its nondescript plumage of greys and dark Rhode Island reds. But its huge and elegantly trailing tail soon dispels all images of poultry.

The lyrebird stamps on its dark trunk platform, uttering short grunts with each convulsive jerk of its body. Suddenly, it raises its great tail and bends it forward to veil its head with a lyre-shaped fan of thin golden feathers framed on each side by a much darker, broader tail feather. The lyrebird shimmers its veil energetically for a few seconds while continuing to call, then repeats the act a few minutes later with equal conviction before slowly backing down the trunk, stamping and calling as it retreats. Then it stops singing in the rain, sleeks its body and drops down into the dense undergrowth of bracken fern.

A female lyrebird, which has been feeding nearby throughout the male's display, emerges from the ferns on the slope and begins to scrape diligently at the litter on the forest floor. Time and again her great claw rakes backward, digging up the surface and exposing crumbly, red soil beneath the debris. Occasionally she reaches down to snap up a minute delicacy that she has uncovered. The female moves calmly up the tree-fern gully, raking here and there, until she reaches a border of ferns. As she ducks under the vegetation she sends a shower of raindrops to the ground.

Lyrebirds are remarkable for more than the males' spectacular if somewhat ostentatious display. The birds breed during the coldest months of the year, with females choosing a partner from among the songsters in the forest before going off alone to do the hard work of reproduction without male participation. Females build the covered nest, a ball of twigs with a central cavity in which is built a cup of fine tree-fern rootlets and downy feathers. The nest is a masterpiece of camouflage, usually set to hug the base of a big tree amid the visual clutter of the wet cool forest of southern Australia.

Females lay a single egg in their nests and single-handedly incubate it for six weeks. When her chick finally appears on the scene, a female has another six weeks of food deliveries ahead before her progeny finally fledges. The three months of solo parenthood is an unusually long period for birds of lyrebird size. Presumably this is why the process must begin in midwinter, for it means that the young will reach independence in spring and summer, the most favorable time for their survival.

The long period of parental care arises in part because the female must do everything herself. She feeds chiefly on minute, soil-dwelling invertebrates and therefore is forced to spend many hours each day tediously scraping and digging in forest litter to find enough prey items to sustain herself. While working to uncover tidbits of food, the female must leave her egg unattended in a winter environment that may be just a few degrees above freezing. An egg left in a nest gradually loses whatever heat it had acquired from its incubating mother and assumes a temperature close to that of the surrounding woodland. Alan Lill found that lyrebirds can abandon their eggs for up to six or seven hours at a stretch. During this time egg temperatures can fall to as low as forty-five degrees Fahrenheit without subsequent developmental damage, quite an achievement for an avian egg. However, although low temperatures do not necessarily damage the embryo, they do slow its development because cell metabolism grinds to a near halt when the egg is cold. The result is delayed hatching.

A male lyrebird could in theory provide his services in the nest-building, incubation, and chick-feeding stages; in over 90 percent of all birds, males provide some parental assistance to their mates. The benefits of aid would seem to be particularly significant for lyrebirds, because if the parents took turns keeping the egg warm it would not be left to grow cold and metabolically inactive for much of each winter's day. The male's help would not only speed egg hatching but would reduce the time a nestling remains vulnerable in the nest by doubling the rate at which food was carried to it. If the egg-laying to fledging time were cut in half, six weeks would be saved, forty-two days in which the discovery of the nest by a predatory marsupial or other deep-forest carnivore would not doom the offspring.

The potential gains of dedicated fatherhood are clear. What costs to males could offset these gains? Here things grow a bit hazy, but perhaps the predator-attraction hypothesis discussed for emancipated bowerbirds applies also to lyrebirds. If two

A male lyrebird displays by shimmering his magnificent tail, which he spreads forward over his head.

adults were going back and forth at the nest, changing incubators, bringing beakfuls of food for the nestling, a predator would have more opportunities to locate a future meal. If the risk of predation were more than doubled, the expected savings in offspring-development time would not be enough to make paternal care reproductively advantageous to the parents. This speculation remains untested, but there is no doubt that predators can find lyrebird nests, even when only one bird slips secretively to and fro. At least 80 percent of all nests in one location were pillaged by predators. Unfortunately, many of these killers were introduced mammals, such as European foxes and cats, and therefore we shall never know how important predation was in the precolonial past when selection shaped the mating system of lyrebirds. But if in the past the danger of nest detection rose sharply with the addition of a second nest attender, it could have been to a female's advantage to dispense with male helping.

Although the reason for the male lyrebird's freedom from parental duties remains uncertain, the evolutionary side effects of the phenomenon have been the same for lyrebirds as for bowerbirds. As is almost universally true for those few birds with nonparental males, lyrebird males produce mating displays that are far more extravagant than those of typical birds, whose males are highly paternal. The traditional explanation for complex species-specific courtship patterns has been that they evolve because females gained by avoiding males of other species; hybrid offspring are often defective and therefore females should prefer males that identify themselves unambiguously as members of the females' own species. But the exceptional vocalizations, the inspired dance, and the elegant tail feathers of an ardent male lyrebird provide more information about species membership than can possibly be needed by even the most befuddled female lyrebird. So the species-identification argument can hardly be the whole story behind the evolution of male lyrebird sexual routines.

Instead we can perhaps invoke the same explanation we used for the exaggerated displays of satin bowerbirds. Although lyrebirds and bowerbirds are placed in different families of birds, they have a common trait—males offer their mates sperm, and sperm only. Because genetic information is all that a female bowerbird or lyrebird can get from their mates, females of these species may require solid evidence that the information is genetically sound. The plumage finery, the strange calls, and the exotic courtship displays of males may in some way convey information about the quality of the performer's genes which females can use to select a partner whose genetic material will help them form successful offspring.

The "good genes" hypothesis, although well known to behavioral scientists, is not yet supported by many demonstrations that females do indeed gain reproductive advantages by mating with some sperm donors as opposed to others. This reflects the great practical difficulties in establishing what it is that females like about displaying males and whether these attributes really are correlated with genetic, developmental, and physiological superiority. I happen to believe that the "good genes" idea is reasonable, but plausibility plays only a partial role in determining the validity of a scientific hypothesis. We must await a rigorous test of the prediction that the offspring of male lyrebirds with special sex appeal will survive, compete, and reproduce better than those fathered by males less favored by females. In the meantime, debate on the issue will continue in scientific circles, while in Australian woodlands male lyrebirds will continue to sing at the top of their lungs and dance to small audiences of skeptical females.

Resin Wasps

Lions of the Insect World

The narrow road to Pearl Beach twists down a steep hillside covered with a jumble of boulders and big yellow-trunked eucalyptus and angophoras. On the slanted face of one boulder, a few yards from the road, female resin wasps have constructed a little patch of brood cells. The translucent cells gleam like stained-glass windows on a sunny day, for they have been built with brilliant orange and red resins collected from oozing trees in the forest. The wasps carry the resin in small round balls, held in jaws that must be made of Teflon, for the droplets are exceptionally sticky. When I touched a resin ball dropped by an incoming female, it formed a superglue bond with my finger and did not let go until I had applied a great deal of soap, hot water, and elbow grease to the spot.

The female wasps handle their tar-baby packages with ease; they stack and mold them into squat, amphora-shaped containers with a pursed entrance that faces out from the rock wall. After the resin dries and hardens a bit, the female will land on the curled lip of her brood cell and crawl inside to suspend

Possible Range of the Resin Wasp

an egg from the ceiling. Later, after the egg has hatched, the mother wasp brings a steady stream of small caterpillars for her hungry grub. When the cell is packed with prey, the female seals the nest entrance with a cover of resin balls. Her larval offspring finishes its development in the red- or orange-tinged twilight of the cell.

Today, as during the previous two weeks, a familiar male perches on the cell cluster. His thorax bears a dot of blue paint as a result of an earlier encounter with me. He wanders about on the beautiful cells, now and then flying out aggressively to chase off incoming visitors of his own sex or to inspect arriving females that are in the midst of building or provisioning a nest.

A group of Aussies on their way to the beach stop and call up from the car to ask with justified bewilderment why on earth I have been perched on the rocky ledge beneath the boulder for the past several weeks. My answer, that I am studying the behavior of a local species of wasp that nests and mates on the rock face, seems to satisfy my questioners, or else to confirm their suspicions about Yanks, as it has for so many other curious passersby over the days of my study. After a bit of chat, during which I try to keep an eye on my wasp charges, the beachgoers head off to their entertainment, leaving me with my less traditional amusement.

For persons interested in the evolution of mating systems, the little resin wasp has much to offer in the way of entertainment. As I watch the wasp I realize that it is a creature whose behavior is analogous to that of such utterly different animals as lions, hamadryas baboons, and zebras, to name a few. In these species, unlike bowerbirds and lyrebirds, females sometimes live in groups, either to exploit their prey more effectively (as in lion prides) or to protect themselves against their enemies (as in baboon troops and zebra herds). Where there are groups of females, there are likely to be some sexually receptive individuals, a harem in waiting. The existence of these ready-made harems creates a special opportunity for competitive males, because the individual that can control access to a group of females will probably have many more chances to copulate and pass on his genes to offspring than a male on the outside. Moreover, if females are grouped together closely, a single male may be able to patrol the boundaries of the harem without excessive expenditure of energy, thereby keeping other males out of the fairly small area occupied by the potential mates in his group. The genetic payoff for a winner is attractive under these conditions, and typically males battle one another with gusto when the reward is a cluster of females. No fancy bowers or dance routines for these males. Instead they fight viciously, with losers regularly injured or even killed in the contests among male baboons and lions.

If the harem-defense strategy occurs in mammals when receptive females are clustered in small, defendable units, the same tactics should be employed in insects that have the same kind of social organization. The resin wasp is a case in point. Because several females may nest in the same location, building many brood cells shoulder to shoulder, a large number of male and female wasps will develop and eventually emerge within a space small enough to be monitored closely by a single territorial male. When a wasp within a cell is ready to enter the external world, it bites little pieces of congealed resin from the cell cap, gradually creating an opening through which it can exit. A resident male can usually detect an emerging wasp in the early stages of cell-cap removal; if the newly adult wasp is a female, the male in charge stations himself by the cell, occasionally intertwining his antennae with the female's, but at times leaving to wander briefly over the cell cluster or to repel a visiting male. The instant the virgin female hauls herself out, the male climbs onto her back and copulates without further ado.

After the two-minute mating is over, a female resin wasp loses her sexual receptivity for the rest of her short life, judging from the response of nesting females to the sexual inspections of resident males. When females mate upon emergence, they receive and store all the sperm they need to fertilize a lifetime's production of eggs. Later they consistently and emphatically reject males that pounce upon them, to the extent of falling from the rock face to roll about on the ground in a successful effort to dislodge their harassers. Therefore, a male's primary, if not only, chance to reproduce comes from contacting virgin females. By far the best location for such contact is at a brood cell when a female is emerging. If a male can defend a cell cluster for several days, he may be able to copulate a number of times, because as many as three females emerged in a single morning during my vigils at Pearl Beach.

Males that monopolize a large cluster of brood cells reap a large reproductive reward. As a result, male resin wasps, like male lions and zebras, compete aggressively to be successful monopolizers of females. A resident resin wasp flies after persistent intruders and strikes them in flight. In a really intense dispute over ownership of a cluster, one male will pounce on

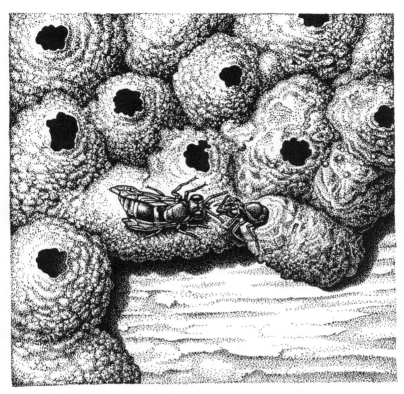

A female resin wasp has begun to gnaw her way out of her brood cell while a territorial male stands nearby, ready to copulate as soon as the female emerges completely.

the other in midair and the two will fall to the ground to wrestle like bully boys in a barroom brawl. They tumble over and over, holding one another with their legs, jabbing with their pseudo-stings (which look like a female's stinger and are located at the tip of the abdomen), and biting forcefully with their mandibles. Marquess of Queensbury rules do not apply. In one fight a combatant lost three legs and an antenna, and in another all-out battle the loser's wing was so mauled that he could no longer fly at the end of the contest.

Just as among squabbling silver gulls, however, most resin wasp disputes are resolved without serious injury. Generally the visitor departs immediately after finding the territory occupied, perhaps because the consequences of losing an all-out fight are so grim. Male resin wasps, like silver gulls, are not violent automatons but can somehow assess their chances of outdueling a rival. If the odds are not good, they assiduously avoid flirtation with early death at the jaws of an opponent. Instead they repeatedly, but cautiously, visit one or more clusters of brood cells, especially during the peak period of female emergence in the early morning, looking for a chance to mate with a virgin that the resident has missed, as happens when an owner gets involved in a territorial argument just as a virgin clambers out of her brood cell. Moreover, territorial males sometimes die, freeing a once-monopolized harem of females. Once I rescued the resident male "blue" from a web a small spider had built in front of the cell cluster; had I not intervened, the wasp would have been killed, providing an opening for one of the more ambitious visitors to the brood cells. The successful replacement would have stalked about on his harem of unemerged females with the confidence of a male lion in his prime surveying the females in his domain.

To perceive basic similarities in the behavior of an obscure little Australian wasp and an African lion is somehow satisfying, and it is even more satisfying to understand that the similarities arise from shared selection pressures. The social environment is fundamentally the same for the wasp and the lion, an environment of intense sexual competition generated by a particular pattern of female distribution. The outcome has been the evolution of lionlike attributes in a wasp, or perhaps we should say the evolution of waspishness in lions.

Water Wasps Down by the Waterhole

The special attraction of the Warrumbungles, home of the hangingflies, brings us there again. The campervan rumbles over the red clay road up into the mountains, a fine dust filtering in; when it rains, the road becomes impassable. For how many roads can we make this claim in the United States? Far too few, for in the U.S.A. journey by car has been sanitized, made too easy, by the almost complete obliteration of dirt roads under seas of asphalt and concrete. It takes an honest effort to get somewhere in much of Australia, but although I admire this point in principle, I do not wish to test the campervan to the limit again and so hope very much that it will not rain heavily during our stay.

At turns in the rutted track we escape the concealing forest and admire black volcanic peaks and spires that push up through the green fabric of ironbarks and monkey gums, stringybarks and bloodwoods.

In the primitive campground a koala occupies a eucalypt adjacent to our parked van. From time to time it showers the

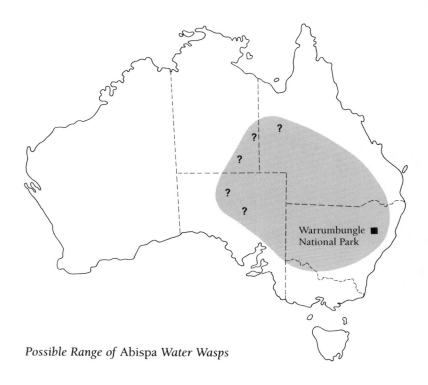

Possible Range of Abispa *Water Wasps*

dried leaf litter with its droppings. Almost all day it sits immobile, propped in a Y-shaped fork in the host tree, dozing in
koalaesque comfort amidst its future meals.

Five red-winged parrots sweep down the narrow glade,
swerving round the crowns of trees, calling sharply as they rush
past. They pull up in a big eucalyptus, whose delicate foliage
frames the perfect combination of luminescent green body
plumage and radiant red wing patches of these magnificent
birds. In the tree with them, noisy friar birds yodel disjointedly,
almost as if they were aware of a need to match their ridiculous
appearance with calls of a suitably clownish nature. A friar bird
peers down with crazed, red-rimmed eyes that gleam from the
blackness of the bird's naked, vulturine head. A black knob
adorns its upper beak, like a pretentious hood ornament on an
overgrown 1950s Oldsmobile.

Beneath the birds the dry bed of Spirey Creek winds down toward abandoned farmland. Farther up the mountain the creek still flows in places, running over sculptured bedrock, forming still pools before moving underground. Nowhere is it more than a few feet wide. Robust orange-and-black wasps, two to three inches long, patrol the water, cruising rapidly around the margins of the larger pools. They swirl about one another when they meet but quickly resume their repetitive journeys. A tiny thornbill flutters to the precious water to drink.

In the Warrumbungles, many streams are impermanent water-courses, for the region is far enough inland to experience long droughts and hot summers. Such water as is available is there-fore the focus of much attention from the smallest to the largest animals. Females of the big striped water wasp need water to construct their nests. They, like the resin wasp, belong to the family Eumenidae; like the resin wasp, they build their brood cells on rocks. But the water wasp uses mud instead of resin to fashion its nests, which are elaborate multichambered complexes that dangle from the roofs of overhangs. To secure mud for her adobe building, a water wasp first fills her crop and then flies to a clay bank where she regurgitates her store of water. With her mandibles she gathers up a jawful of water-softened mud of the right consistency and then sails back to the nest site to add a load to her growing nest. To finish the nest the female adds a trumpet-shaped opening that points to the earth. The wasp will travel through this opening with prey to feed her offspring within the mud-walled labyrinth she has built.

Female water wasps differ from resin wasps in two important ways. They do not nest in groups, and they apparently retain their sexual receptivity throughout their lives, rather than mating just once after emergence. These factors taken together have major consequences for male reproductive tactics, if we assume that males should behave in ways that will help them leave as many descendants as possible. The harem-defense strategy that works so well for some male resin wasps is ill-suited for water wasps. A male of this species that guarded a nest to mate with freshly emerged virgins would wind up with

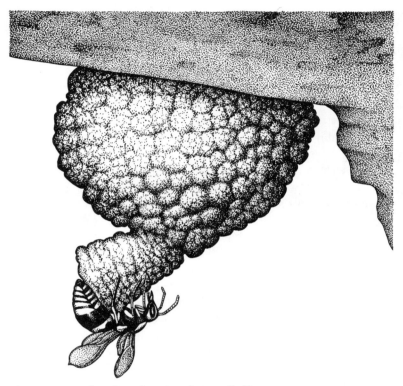

A water wasp female at her complex mudball nest.

relatively few mates, because one nest has a limited number of brood cells and half of these will yield males eventually. Even more importantly, when his partners mated again (and female water wasps copulate with any male that can capture them at any stage in their adulthood), the new male's sperm would displace or dilute any sperm stored within them earlier. A nest-guarding male would gain few offspring in all likelihood from his copulations. Thus, although resin and water wasps are fellow eumenids, water wasp males face different obstacles to reproductive success and we can predict that they should have evolved different techniques for getting mates. And they have.

Male water wasps take advantage of the females' need to drink water for making mud. Limited water sources concentrate females in small areas, and males can profitably patrol pools searching for them. When a male detects an arriving, departing, or drinking female, he swoops down to land on her back. If he can grasp the female, he flies with his unresisting partner to a tree near the stream, although if she is drinking when he pounces he generously permits her to fill her crop before carrying her off to the nuptial tree. Once in the foliage they mate briefly, and then the female is released to go about her business.

I strongly suspect that a male's primary chance to fertilize an egg comes when his mate happens to return to her nest to complete a brood cell and lay an egg within, without an intervening copulation. If she fertilizes the egg with the stored sperm of her last partner, which is the common rule among insects, the lucky last male will gain a potential descendant.

By mating with as many females as possible, and some of my marked males copulated at least four times in one afternoon, a male may occasionally hit the genetic jackpot. This system favors indefatigable males with the capacity to patrol stream pools for hours on end in a keen-eyed search for members of the opposite sex. Because the Warrumbungle pools were large, males could not defend them easily and they made no effort to do so as they traveled past other searching males in a circular race to be first to find a female.

A potential alternative would be for a male to take up "monogamous" residence with one female at her nest, copulating every time she returned in order to supplant sperm she might have received from other males while on water-collecting missions. Some males of a species very closely related to my water wasps do exactly this. In theory the comparative profitability of the monogamy and water-searching options would depend on a number of factors, such as the degree to which males can supersede the sperm of earlier rivals, the ease with which nesting females can be found, and the rate of contacts with females at limited water sources. There is every reason to expect that male water wasps are unconsciously adept mathematicians, rather like New Holland honeyeaters, when it comes to making decisions about critical issues in their lives. Perhaps some day someone will demonstrate that males of this wasp, like males of many other insects, have the ability to employ more than one mating tactic depending on the local conditions they experience.

But we never expect to find male water wasps exercising a decided preference for virgins, unlike their distant cousins the resin wasps. Evolutionary theory predicts that male wasps, like male lions and zebras, should evolve behavioral capacities that offer the greatest reproductive return for them as individuals. The difference in the behavior of male water wasps and resin wasps is consistent with this expectation, for although they are of similar ancestry, they have diverged remarkably in their mating behavior in a manner related to differences in the ecology of their females. The separate tactics they employ illustrate powerfully that a male's life revolves and evolves around competition for females, whose attributes and distribution dictate the rules of the game.

Primitive or Degenerate?

The marsupials stand in many important characters below the placental mammals. They appear at an earlier geological period, and their range was formerly much more extensive than at present. Hence the Placentata are generally supposed to have been derived from the . . . Marsupials; not, however, from forms closely resembling the existing marsupials, but from their early progenitors.

Charles Darwin

Cassowaries

Primitive, Not Degenerate

In a swamp below Picton Hill, three red-eyed drongos sit in black silhouette on a white paperbark limb. In Aussie slang to call someone a drongo is not to heap praise on that person, for the term implies a kind of flaky, oddball stupidity. So I watch the drongos with interest to see if they live up to their reputation. Which they do, by taking turns at plunging headfirst into a shallow, grassy puddle thirty feet beneath them, like high-school boys on a dare at the swimming hole. This is a drongo version of taking a bath because although they appear to be headed precipitously for a broken neck, they pull out of their dives just as they hit the surface of the pool and fly back with drenched plumage to their perches. There the birds shake their jet-black feathers with a swaggering flourish, sending a shower of droplets back into the water below.

The track on Picton Hill climbs slowly up forested slopes with a riotous understory of broad-leaved jungle plants. From a lookout on the hill the Queensland coast appears below, flat and checkered with freshly plowed red rectangles cut in the

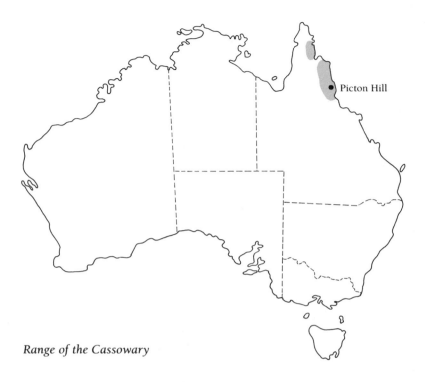

Range of the Cassowary

rich green cloth of the landscape. Two boats loaded with tourists leave insignificant wakes in the tropical blue water of the
Pacific.

The trail circles back from the lookout around the hill, cutting across slopes so steep that most of the soil has washed
away, allowing only a few trees and palms to retain a foothold.
Here the forest is open and uncluttered. The thin palms soar
upward to a canopy of fringed symmetrical fan leaves; lianas
descend smoothly in the spaces between trees.

Heavy footsteps intrude on the silence of the forest, coming
toward me from behind a little rise on the hillside just ahead.
Who could be cutting across country in this terrain? The
puzzle resolves itself when a cassowary every bit as big as I am
steps into the open and crosses the path a few paces from me.

The horny helmet on its head is chipped and worn from years of pushing through jungle tangles. The long red wattles on its neck swing incongruously as it walks.

The cassowary's feathers look like fine black hairs, and a great mound of them are heaped on the bird's huge back. The nape of its neck is a powdery baby blue, a soft color at odds with the preponderance of fierce blacks and grim greys in its plumage and out of keeping with the bird's reputation as a killer of men. The most discussed features of the bird are its specially modified, daggerlike inner toes, which cassowaries are said to exercise occasionally on human beings that get in their way. An exotic death by disembowelment, one to be avoided, one that tops death from snake bite, shark attack, spider assault, sea wasp sting, and the poisonous stab of a cone shell, all tickets to the next world which can be bought in Australia.

The cassowary serenely ignores its lethal reputation and me as it plods downhill, planting first one elephantine foot and then the other in the debris on the steep slope. A thin barbed trailer of a creeper palm catches under its chin, and the big bird jerks its head back to escape the bite of the thorns.

Although a cassowary's toes may be its most lurid attribute, its flightlessness is a good deal more intriguing from an evolutionary perspective. A long-debated question in ornithology has been whether cassowaries and other giant flightless birds such as ostriches and emus are descended relatively recently from more or less modern flying birds, or whether they are descendants of an ancient lineage that either never had the ability to fly or else lost it very early in the history of birds. A firm answer appeared in 1984 on a cover of the scientific journal *Nature* with the bold proclamation, "Ostriches primitive, not degenerate."

At first glance this may seem faint praise for ostriches, although who would not prefer to be called primitive rather than degenerate. The editors of *Nature*, however, were not passing moral judgment on ostriches. Indeed, they wished only to draw attention (and they succeeded in my case) to an article appearing in that issue of the journal. In it, Christopher McGowan concluded that ostriches and other flightless species, or *ratites*, all of which lack a keeled breastbone for the attachment of flight muscles, are primitive in that they have a very long evolutionary history separate from modern flying birds. They are not degenerate in the sense of having lost the capacity for flight after they had achieved it in near-modern form.

The key evidence in support of McGowan's conclusion comes not from the discovery of fossil ostrichlike birds but from a comparison of the development of living species. By taking X-rays of the leg bones of various flightless and flying birds during the early stages of their embryonic development, McGowan found two very different patterns. Flying birds, like drongos, have a distinctive "pretibial bone" that fuses with the calcaneum, another leg bone, whereas the ostrich, the cassowary, and other ratites have an "ascending process" that fuses with the astragalus, a different leg bone. The resulting ratite leg has the same components as the legs of extinct theropod dinosaurs, a nice bit of evidence for the evolutionary link between birds and reptiles.

The great difference in leg structure between ratites and flying birds makes it highly unlikely that these two groups had a recent common ancestor, for if they had they would have inherited the same pattern of tarsal development.

After the publication of McGowan's report, another article in *Nature* provided a completely independent line of evidence supporting the hypothesis of separate evolutionary histories for ratites and modern flighted birds. A group of Dutch molecular biologists analyzed the sequence of amino acid building blocks that constitute the protein α-crystalline A, a molecule that makes up much of the lens of vertebrate eyes. All proteins consist of chains of various amino acids hooked together, one after the other. It is possible to identify the order of amino acids in a protein, and when the Dutch scientists did this for α-crystalline A taken from the lenses of emus, rheas, and ostriches, they found them to be all but identical. But the ratite sequence differs sharply from that of flying birds and is actually more similar to the reptilian sequence as represented by alligator α-crystalline A. This similarity points again to an evolutionary connection between birds and reptiles and strongly suggests that the ancestor of modern ratites split off from the evolutionary line from reptiles to birds very early on in the game, before the origin of those birds that gave rise eventually to modern flying species.

The story gets a bit complicated, thanks to yet another molecular study, this one involving an analysis by Charles Sibley and Jon Ahlquist of the DNA of the ratites and other birds. The DNA molecule carries the genes of living things, and therefore

A cassowary walking through the rainforest.

the discovery of ways to measure precisely the degree of similarity between the DNAs of two species is a powerful aid in determining how recently they shared a common ancestor from whom they inherited their genes. I have more to say about this technique in an upcoming chapter, but for the moment it is enough to say that the DNA study confirms that ratites have very different DNA than that of most flying birds—except for the tinamous. These quail-like birds of South America spend most of their time walking on the ground in the concealment of thick cover, but they are perfectly capable of flying. Sibley and Ahlquist consider tinamous to be ratites, based on the fact that their DNA is far more like that of rheas and ostriches than that of any other flying birds.

If correct, the DNA study raises the possibility that the ancient ancestor of the cassowary and tinamous could fly, but that flight has been lost in most ratites and retained in tinamous. In other words, cassowaries and ostriches are indeed primitive in that the ancestor of these birds (and the tinamous) appeared in the world well before the bird species that gave rise to all modern flying birds except tinamous. But the flightless ratites might also be degenerate if they lost the ability to fly long, long ago.

No one knows for sure whether the proto-ostrich/cassowary could fly, or who the ratite ancestors of this creature may have been, or how closely related they were to *Archaeopteryx*, the most famous fossil bird of all. The detective work needed to reconstruct the complete evolutionary history of the flightless cassowary probably requires that missing fossil bones be found, dated, and placed in their proper relationships with other fossils. This will be accomplished eventually, luck permitting, but even without this evidence, I am impressed by how much we already know about the evolution of the cassowary, thanks to the right kinds of comparisons among *living* species. Although the development of various techniques for comparing current birds may be still in a fairly primitive stage, the general approach has already advanced our ability to decipher a portion of the past from the present.

The Bad Rap on Marsupials

Verdict of a Kangaroo Court?

With my sabbatical teaching responsibilities at Monash nearly completed and spring well advanced, I load the campervan for a one-man expedition into New South Wales, a warm-up for a much more ambitious journey I will be taking with my family shortly. My route to Willandra National Park, in south-central New South Wales, takes me though Googoolwi, Merriwagga, and finally a village with the uninspired name of Hillston, a place with two gas stations at the end of the paved part of the road. The "unsealed" road toward the edge of the outback begins with an ominous sign—"Strictly Dry Weather Road." It is extremely dry, and a fine grey dust boils up behind the van, an enormous dinosaur's tail of pulverized earth that streams after the car as it tears across the flat grey field running to the horizon at every point of the compass. Three large plovers stand stolidly on the hard-packed plain; a broad, black chest band disrupts the muted white-and-brown outfit of each bird.

The road continues west in a single-minded way, not swerving or bending, but plowing straight ahead in a futile effort to

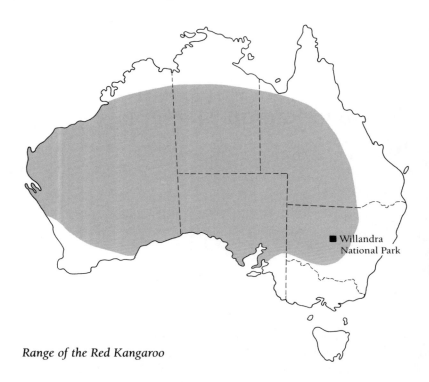

■ Willandra
National Park

Range of the Red Kangaroo

outrun the desolate and desiccated landscape. A side track
eventually runs into Willandra Station, whose sweeps of pasture had been grazed by sheep from the mid-nineteenth century until only a few years ago. Now the Park Service attempts,
without much success as yet, to restore the land to its pregraz-
ing state.

   The Park caretaker is out by Billabong Creek, spraying the
toxic herbicide 2–4D on burdock, trying to kill this European
weed inadvertently introduced into Australia. Although the native plants are withered browns, greys, and whitish greens, the
rank, radiantly green burdock is doing insultingly well on the
borders of the Billabong. The herbicidal spray stinks horrifi-
cally of petrochemicals and turns the brown stagnant water of
the creek an unnatural milky white.

Near this scene of plant versus man, a family of white-winged blue wrens springs from one saltbush to another, defying the intense heat of midday. A male with luminescent blue body and spotless white wings perches for a moment on the outer twigs of a shrub before plunging into its shade.

Little else stirs in the heat except for bands of grasshoppers. Everywhere there are mobs, armies of hoppers intent on demolishing the last vestiges of green grass. The hard-packed mud track sparkles with reflections from the cellophane wings of thousands of crushed insects. Hundred of thousands of survivors are on the move, leapfrogging their way across the prairie, filling the air with the sibilant whirring of their wings.

As an unwanted bonus, there are bush flies, too, each one an insignificant creature in itself, incapable of biting, a small, drab, black insect that would not be worth a second glance were it not for one thing—sheer numbers. They come to me by the dozens and by the hundreds, armed only with infinite patience and an unquenchable desire to inspect my body and especially my face. They march up the inner surface of the lenses of my glasses, creating a Kafkaesque vision before my very eyes; they crawl into my eyes, my ears, my nose, my mouth, returning again and again when waved away, searching for moisture with awesome dedication to the job. They cannot be defeated, only endured.

The stale, muddy water of the creek has begun to evaporate. Shallow sloughs lie drying beneath the sun, surrounded by a narrow fringe of trees. A pied butcherbird, a handsome black-and-white shrike with a cruelly hooked butcher's bill, sings in the shaded canopy. Slater's field guide says that one of its songs recalls the opening bars of Beethoven's Fifth Symphony.

A pair of red kangaroos rests in the middle of a dry ex-slough, taking advantage of the precarious shade of a single dead eucalyptus. The massive reddish-brown male has wide muscle-bound shoulders and thick upper arms; he looks sluggish beside the much smaller and more graceful female. Flies swirl around them. The female dejectedly shakes her head, ears flopping, eyes partly closed, a picture of resignation.

In the early evening, before a night wind rattles the drying grasses, kangaroos bound out of their resting places in the scrub to feed warily in the open fields. The heartless flies are far fewer now. Grasshoppers and aboriginal stone flake tools rest on the dark red clay of a dry pan under the darkening sky.

Because relatively few visitors come to isolated Willandra, the red kangaroos have not lost their fear of humans, unlike their jaded cousins in some other national parks. Because it was so recently a working sheep station, kangaroos in and around Willandra were almost surely shot regularly until a few years ago. Between 1960 and 1969, 1,358,000 kangaroos were killed legally in New South Wales and no doubt a great many more were dispatched illegally during the same period. Most were destroyed because they, like sheep, consume grass and so compete for forage the ranchers wished to reserve for their domesticated charges.

In the year that I visited Willandra there was a ban (since lifted) on the importation of kangaroo products into the United States. Without the U.S. market for kangaroo leather, a hide's value had fallen to about $4.00, not enough to make it worthwhile to hunt kangaroos. The caretaker at Willandra claimed wistfully that if only the ban were rescinded, the value of a kangaroo skin would hit $60.00. He was prepared to take advantage of the opportunity if it presented itself.

The caretaker represented rural Australians well in his lack of affection for kangaroos. Although roos may symbolize the country to foreigners, to Australian farmers the animal symbolizes grass down the wrong gullet, and money down the drain. Biologists, Australian or otherwise, tend to view kangaroos more charitably than outback station inhabitants, admiring, for example, the stunning diversity of these marsupials, which range from little pademelons to chunky wallabies and shaggy euros to big grey and red kangaroos. In the tropical north of Queensland, there are even tree kangaroos, elegant golden-brown creatures that scramble about in trees, of all places.

A large male and smaller female red kangaroo racing over an Australian plain.

But until the mid-1970s most biologists accepted the argument that kangaroos and their marsupial kin were as a group inferior in important ways to placental mammals. The attitude that marsupials are second-rate mammals, more primitive, less fully developed, a taxonomic backwater, comes first from the evidence that marsupials evolved earlier than mammals. Second, there is the plausible argument that they are dominant in Australia only because they were sheltered from competition with placentals, thanks to the isolation afforded by their island continent. Supporters of this position point to the extinction of many marsupials in Australia after the modern introduction of some placental species, most importantly the dingo. The same thing happened millions of years ago in South America, when many species of marsupials there disappeared following an invasion of North American placental mammals that crossed over the newly formed land bridge in Panama. One interpretation of the wave of extinction is that placental mammals outcompeted the less capable marsupials.

One trouble with this argument, however, is that some marsupials are doing just fine, thanks, both in South and North America as well as in Australia, despite the presence of placental mammals on these continents. In addition, the proportion of South American placental mammals that went extinct at the time of the great North American influx was essentially the same as the proportion of marsupials that bit the dust. The die-off of South American placental animals should give pause to those who hold that there is something inherently superior about the competitive ability associated with the placental mode of reproduction. Bobbi Low asks us, therefore, to consider the possibility that the reproductive strategies of marsupials may be different but as fully adaptive as those of placental mammals.

To illustrate this counterview, let's compare the reproductive strategy of a typical marsupial, such as the big red kangaroo, with that of a typical placental, the white-tailed deer. A female red kangaroo nurtures a single offspring at a time, giving birth after just thirty-three days to an infant that weighs less than one gram, far less than the weight of an airmail letter. Upon entering the world, the minuscule naked creature has the ability to crawl from the birth canal opening to the maternal pouch, a long and difficult journey over the fur of its mother. Within the marsupium, it attaches to a teat and undergoes the rest of its development outside its mother, rather than as an internal embryo. Shortly after giving birth, the female becomes sexually receptive, mates, and holds the zygote that results from fertilization of the egg in a state of suspended animation (*delayed implantation*) until such time as she no longer has an older offspring under her care. This may be many months down the road, if all goes well. But should she lose her joey prematurely, she can begin at once to activate embryonic development and will give birth to a replacement in about one month. This is a decidedly sophisticated system, and not obviously inferior to the placental mode, merely different.

A placental mammal such as a white-tailed deer has an alternative reproductive cycle. After mating and egg fertilization, the zygote becomes implanted in the uterus and is sustained by a complex placental organ that permits the exchange of blood and nutrients from mother to offspring. The gestation of a deer, an animal about the same size as a red kangaroo, lasts six times as long, and the newborn fawn weighs three thousand times as much as a newborn joey. It follows that the period of postnatal parental care is considerably shorter for a mother deer. White-tailed deer do not mate promptly after giving birth, but instead have a well-defined breeding season; nor do deer employ the delayed implantation technique.

Given these clearcut differences between kangaroo and deer, we can ask under what environmental conditions would the marsupial pattern be superior. Low points out that the climate of the Australian interior offers special challenges that are effectively solved by marsupials. The vast majority of Australia qualifies as a desert; that which is not formally desert is highly arid except for a narrow coastal strip. Most significantly, the intervals between rains in the dry regions of Australia are exceptionally unpredictable. A red kangaroo in the outback can have no guarantee that conditions favorable for the survival of her youngster will persist over the months needed for its full development. Devastating drought could settle in at any time. By giving birth so "prematurely," a female kangaroo avoids the costs of preparing a complex placenta, and she avoids the risks associated with giving birth to a large-bodied neonate. If drought conditions make it impossible to sustain a current offspring, she can end her parental investment simply by removing the joey from her pouch. The placental mammal must undergo a spontaneous abortion, with all the physiological dangers attendant on this mode of terminating an unsuccessful reproductive attempt, risks that are especially great when a fetus reaches a relatively large size. Incidentally, the use of a marsupium also enables a kangaroo female, hard pressed by a predator, to jettison her cargo of offspring, an extreme choice but one that may save the female for several more chances to reproduce in the future.

The critical point is that the marsupial approach permits a female to make a very small commitment during the period from conception to birth, facilitating a termination in parental care for any one offspring should this be advantageous in terms of her lifetime output of surviving young. By cutting her losses so effectively and easily, a female marsupial is in position to make more lifetime attempts at reproduction in a gambler's environment than are placental females, which must devote a great proportion of their parental investment in offspring *in utero*. Always having an embryo in delayed implantation also helps the marsupial maximize her reproductive output, for she can respond to an unexpected loss quickly.

Our tendency to view other species as more or less "advanced" in proportion to their similarity to ourselves is partly responsible for our traditional high regard for placentalism and corresponding depreciation of the "primitive" marsupial mode. The variety of environments in the world makes room for both types of mammalian reproductive approaches, and I doubt that one can be labeled innately better than the other.

On my way back to Melbourne from Willandra I stayed the night in a grim little caravan park at Rankin's Springs, a sort of Appalachian hamlet in the middle of nowhere. Upon returning from the moldering showerblock to fix my supper, I found a portly older man dressed in faded grey slacks, thongs, and a sleeveless undershirt inspecting the campervan with interest. A temporary caravan park neighbor, he wanted to talk. I wanted to get supper on the table. We compromised; he talked and I fixed supper. In the course of his monologue he asked me where I had been that day, and I replied, "Willandra." My answer induced a toothless smile; he and his father had stayed at Willandra Station long ago, his father as a shearer. He sat and talked while I had my supper. He had eaten already and he also turned down a beer, saying cheerfully that he was a religious man, as his father had been before him. His name was Duncan Ferguson and he was one-quarter aborigine because both parents had some aboriginal blood. He had first worked as a low-paid servant boy at Roto Station, which I had passed in the dust earlier that day. He had been paid seven and a half shillings a week for his work.

Before the conversation slowed and we parted company, he told me about a time he and his father had constructed a kangaroo trap in the scrub far to the north of Rankin's Springs. They put out poisoned water in two large drums near a natural well where the animals came to drink. Kangaroos drank the stuff and died. He and his father located the dead animals, skinned them out, and in the end sent out bales of stiff hides by truck. He spoke with some remorse about the trickery of poisoning thirsty kangaroos, for the unfairness of it bothered him a little.

We chatted until it was dark and the stars and a few mosquitoes came out, and then we said good night, my mood much improved by supper and our conversation. During the night thousands of kangaroos disported themselves in the bush and wheatfields about Rankin's Springs. Red and grey kangaroos have reproduced so successfully that they are almost surely much more abundant now than they were prior to the arrival in Australia of that most potent placental predator, European man. The spread of agriculture and the drilling of stock wells have created a bonanza much appreciated and much exploited by the resident roos. "Primitive" they may be in the eyes of some, but their reproductive physiology and behavior have enabled them to flourish even in the face of culling quotas in the millions per year, poisoned wells, handbag projects, and dog-food schemes. After all this they can cope with an insult or two.

Duck-Billed Platypus

Not a Relict, Not a Reject

Most of the national parks and forest reserves of Queensland are scattered along the coast wherever chance or rough terrain has prevented the destruction of the subtropical forest. We punctuate the long drive up the coast with stops in these fragmentary islands of jungle vegetation in a discouraging sea of pastures, sugarcane fields, resorts, and towns.

At Eungella the dirt road skirts the edge of a ribbon of rainforest still surviving on an escarpment overlooking coastal lowlands now devoted almost exclusively to agriculture. The road ducks down a hill, runs past a simple campground, and swings up and over a discolored, slow-moving stream. From the bridge one can look down on a quiet pool bordered by a fringe of luxuriant vegetation.

The trail by the bridge slides into the quiet forest and parallels the stream. A recent rain has left the leaf mold black and wet. A bracket fungus shines with moist alternating bands of black and yellow. By the water's edge, strange palmlike trees spread their crowns of flat long leaves overtopping thin trunks.

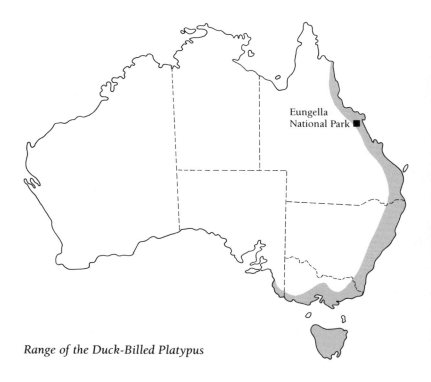

Eungella
National Park ■

Range of the Duck-Billed Platypus

The creek tumbles down a rocky incline and then resumes its customary sluggish pace. Banks overhang the water in a tangle of exposed roots and dark soil. A platypus emerges from under a bank and dogpaddles calmly through the water, looking like a mutant muskrat. Its great broad bill pushes ahead while the creek flows around its brown body.

The platypus and two other animals, the Australian spiny anteater, or echidna, and a New Guinea echidna, constitute the monotremes, a group distinguished by their ability to lay eggs. Monotreme eggs would not be worth shouting about were it not for the fact that the platypus and echidnas are indisputably mammals. Anyone watching a furry platypus paddling along, its big beaver tail floating behind, can have little doubt about this. Moreover, the animal not only possesses a mammalian pelt, but also mammary glands with which females nourish their young, although the mammaries are so inconspicuous that they are difficult to find even when one can inspect a female's belly at close range, something that I did not have the chance to do at Eungella or elsewhere.

What is easily seen by a streamside observer is the impressive platypus bill, which is not at all like the bony, keratinous bill of a bird but instead is a soft and flexible appendage composed largely of cartilage. With its delicate bill the platypus feels out and snuffles up bottom-dwelling insects, crayfish, and sunken earthworms in dark and murky waters. And the platypus is something of a gourmand, judging from a captive specimen's daily consumption of a pound of earthworms, dozens of mealworms, plus assorted crayfish, frogs, and two coddled eggs.

Most of the truly exceptional features of the platypus are still poorly understood, for few people have studied the details of its reproductive biology. Even the basic social system of the animal remains largely mysterious. But observations of marked individuals have revealed that some platypus stay in home pools, never more than one male to a pool with one or more resident females. This suggests that male platypus, like male resin wasps and lions, engage in harem defense. Moreover, mature males weigh as much as 75 percent more than mature females. Throughout the animal kingdom, when males are much heavier than females, the mating system is usually one in which males are pugilists in competition for groups of females. In addition, male platypus, and males alone, have a spur on the heel of the hind leg through which they can inject venom from a poison gland in the thigh, an ability that makes handling the animal problematic for human captors. But if the main function of the apparatus were to protect a platypus against predators, one would expect both males and females to possess it. That only males can "sting" indicates that they use the weapon primarily in dealings with one another, a conclusion strengthened by the finding that the volume of the poison gland increases during the breeding season.

When females are receptive, males probably fight for mates and the winners are rewarded with copulations. Mothers-to-be retire to hidden bankside tunnels that they do not share with a male. There they lay one to three eggs while resting on a nest of grass and leaves at the end of a burrow that may be fifty feet long. For years I imagined a platypus egg to be as big as a hen's egg, but in reality the monotreme egg is a tiny thing, less than one inch long, a fact discovered by H. W. Caldwell only a century ago.

When a female gives birth to her small eggs they stick to each other and to the hairs on the female's abdomen. An incubating female curls her tail over her eggs and remains nestbound for about a week until the eggs finally hatch. The naked, tiny platypus infant enters the world by breaking the shell in the fashion of many birds, with a special egg tooth on its upper mandible. It is then nurtured by milk from the mother's mammary glands, which ooze fluid onto the surface of her belly, there to be lapped up by her infants. It will be four months before the young are fully enough developed to leave their burrow for the first time.

An egg-laying mammal is a wonderful anomaly. Anatomical studies of fossil vertebrates in conjunction with procedures for dating the rocks in which they appear show beyond reasonable doubt that reptiles evolved before mammals and that the first mammals were highly similar to reptiles, so much so that the distinction between them at this stage is largely semantic. The existence of monotremes provides yet another small piece of evidence in support of this evolutionary view, for they have evidently retained one reptilian characteristic, egg-laying, despite possessing a host of undeniably mammalian traits.

This does not mean that the platypus is an inefficiently primitive mammal that lacks the refinements of less reptilian species. Just as we argued that marsupials are not inherently inferior mammals, so too the platypus and the echidna are superbly adapted to their environment. For example, it has been discovered that the platypus has the capacity to detect very weak electric fields, an ability that humans lack but that comes in handy when searching for food at the bottom of a muddy

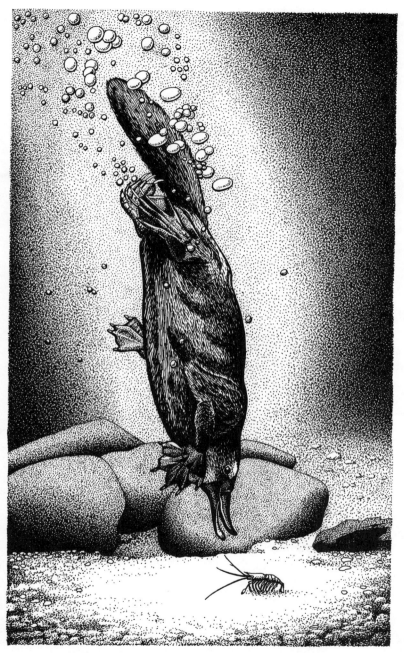

A diving platypus armed with the capacity to sense faint electrical cues emanating from the freshwater shrimp that it will capture and eat.

stream. Because prey animals inadvertently produce a weak electric field, the specialized perceptual ability to detect this stimulus enables platypus and some other aquatic predators to find food in environments such as muddy creeks where visual detection of prey is out of the question.

The egg-laying tactics of monotremes are probably adaptive, too, although this remains to be examined in detail. As is true for marsupials, the female monotreme is not burdened by a huge internal embryo, birth is uncomplicated and carries little risk, and an investment in reproduction can be canceled simply and quickly under unfavorable conditions by abandoning the immature young rather than by a dangerous spontaneous abortion.

The highly evolved state of the platypus is further reflected in the difficulty specialists have in identifying its precise historical relationships with other mammals. Time and natural selection did not stop for the monotremes; they do not constitute a little slice of evolutionary history taken early in the transition from ancestral reptile to modern mammals and held in deep freeze in an Australian museum until the present. While retaining one early-evolved characteristic, egg laying, they have continued to change in a host of ways that are apparent in the extraordinary differences in appearance and lifestyle between the aquatic platypus, a Jacques Cousteau of its world, and the spiny echidna, a terrestrial pincushion. As a result of the multiplicity of evolutionary changes that have occurred over the millennia, there is doubt about who might be the closest relatives of monotremes; some specialists profess to see an affinity with the marsupials, whereas others argue with equal tenacity that monotremes split from the mammalian lineage long before the first marsupials appeared. This dispute need not concern us, except to confirm that the platypus and echidnas have a history that is as long and involved as that of any other currently existing mammal, a history with magnificent results.

A Once and Future Possum?

We walk through a somber twilight forest of immense eucalyptus, mountain ashes, whose thick trunks shoot up two hundred, even three hundred feet, the envy of California redwood foresters. The biggest trees support a ridiculously scanty collection of leaf-bearing branches far, far above the ground. Many big trees in the Marysville area have not yet been cut, although mountain ash throughout its range in eastern Australia has come under extreme pressure from the lumber industry.

The trail leads to a nest tree of the Leadbeater's possum, a little arboreal marsupial that looks for all the world like a squirrel and behaves like one, too. The possums favor dead mountain ash with large rot cavities that they fill with insulating shredded bark to make a safe, relatively warm shelter in which several animals may spend their inactive hours sleeping. Winter nights are cold in the mountains of Victoria, and the little marsupials conserve body heat through communal roosting in their bark-filled shelters.

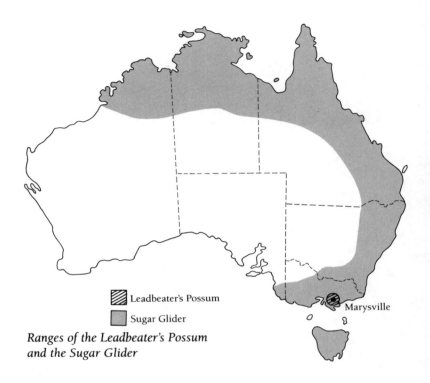

Leadbeater's Possum

Sugar Glider

Marysville

Ranges of the Leadbeater's Possum and the Sugar Glider

Just as Andrew Smith, a student of Leadbeater's possums, has predicted, first one and then another and another of the squirrel-like creatures come scampering from their shelter in the chilly evening. They make their way to a trailside wattle tree, much smaller than many of the surrounding mountain ashes. Because it is growing in something of a clearing created by the trail and the fall of a monster ash, the wattle has an abundance of foliage. The possums bound with confidence along its limbs; they know where they are going, having visited the tree many times before to feed on sugary exudates that ooze from wounds in the bark. Although the possums enjoy insects when they can get them, they rely heavily on carbohydrate-rich secretions from trees such as wattles, which grow in the understory of the mountain ash forest.

As the darkness grows, the Leadbeater's possums become more and more difficult to follow. Their gradual disappearance is somehow appropriate for an animal that is considered an endangered species, thanks to the destruction of the mature mountain ash forests on which the possum depends. Modern forestry practices involve the cutting of "overmature" trees and the removal of dead stubs that use up space that might otherwise be employed in growing living trees for future harvests. But the possums need the dead trees for their nest homes, and without warm shelters the animals face a cold future.

The problem for Leadbeater's possums is compounded by the fact that the animal has always been rare and restricted to a very small region in Australia. For about forty years it was even considered extinct, but happily in 1961 it was rescued from premature oblivion when some animals were rediscovered in the Marysville area. It remains to be seen whether they will be placed again in the extinct category, this time for keeps.

Although not a dramatically exotic animal, the extinction of Leadbeater's possum would be a shame; the animal is a pleasure to have around, for many reasons. For one thing, the species provides a fine example of a characteristic Australian phenomenon, namely, convergence between marsupalian and placental mammals. Leadbeater's possum is to all intents and purposes a squirrel, but one that has evolved independently from a marsupial ancestor, not from the placental mammal that evolved into the arboreal squirrels that Americans know well. The original marsupial that occupied Australia many millions of years ago founded a lineage that yielded a complete set of ecological analogues to the placental mammals that evolved in other continents. There are (or were) marsupial wolves and lions, squirrels and rats, marmots and sloths, shrews and anteaters, moles and flying squirrels.

Speaking of flying marsupials, Leadbeater's possum also has something to tell us about how these animals came about, because the little possum provides clues to the adaptive radiation that has taken place within its family, the Petauridae. Leadbeater's possum is another "primitive" animal whose relatively "simple" body plan is presumed to be similar to that of an ancestral species of some most unusual petaurids, the sugar glider and the yellow-bellied glider. These close relatives of Leadbeater's possum are, as the name "glider" implies, aerial mammals capable of sailing from one tree to the next like the unrelated North American flying squirrel. When at rest, a sugar glider's affinities to the Leadbeater's possum are obvious, for the two species are very similar in their squirrel-like appearance. But unlike the "primitive" possum, the sugar glider possesses a flap of skin that stretches between fore and hind legs and which when extended converts the glider into a furry parachute of a marsupial.

Thanks to the assistance of Graeme Suckling, then a graduate student at Monash engaged in research on the sugar glider, we had the pleasure of watching the animal in action. As part of his study Graeme had placed a number of honey-baited traps in an open woodland in southern Victoria where the animals were common. In the morning he retrieved captured gliders that were waiting honey-filled in their box traps. Almost all were marked animals, individuals whose life histories were partly known to Graeme. He checked the reproductive status of each one, showing us a female with two minute naked babies attached to teats in her marsupium.

After having released all but a couple of his gliders, Graeme took one to a tall dead eucalyptus in an opening in the woodland pasture. As soon as the sugar glider had left its trap it raced up the dead tree until it was about thirty feet above the ground. It then turned and hurled itself into space, legs stretched apart to the maximum, and with its gliding membranes fully deployed it sailed across the clearing. As it traveled the glider lost altitude but far less rapidly than it would have without its parachute, and it was still airborne when it reached a tree some fifty to sixty feet from its starting point. It landed with a thump, belly to bark, and sprinted up eucalyptus number two, using it as another launching pad for another "flight" to yet another tree, this one within the black box eucalyptus

Two sugar gliders climbing on a tree trunk. Although these animals superficially resemble squirrels, they are marsupials. The loose fold of skin on the side of the animal becomes a gliding membrane when the sugar glider leaps from a tree with its legs extended.

woodland where it lived. In a matter of seconds the glider had disappeared into the safety of its daytime retreat.

Thanks to the existence of Leadbeater's possum, it is not too difficult to imagine how gliding ability might have evolved in an ancestor of the sugar glider. A squirrel-like ancestor that happened to have a wider-than-average flap of skin between its fore and hind legs would have probably been able to glide just a bit further when jumping from limb to limb than the average

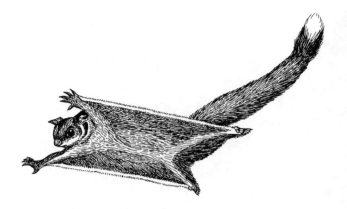

individual in its population. If this gave the gliding individual an added safety margin when falling or expanded its foraging range even slightly, the trait could have become established, serving as the foundation for additional modifications over time and resulting eventually in a superb gliding machine. Sugar gliders can inhabit fairly open woodland without ever needing to descend to the ground where their predators would like to meet them.

The advantages of gliding for an arboreal mammal are such that not only has gliding evolved independently in petaurid marsupials and North American placentals but also independently in two other families of Australian marsupials. The greater glider, a member of the family Pseudocheiridae and a much bigger animal than the sugar glider, feeds on eucalyptus leaves in the treetops; the tiny feather-tailed glider, a member of the Burramyidae, consumes nectar, pollen, acacia exudates, and the like in dense forests in eastern Australia.

The capacity of evolutionary processes to produce the same adaptive solution to a similar ecological problem over and over again from different starting points offers unusually strong evidence about the power of natural selection. The genetic and developmental systems of the ancestors of greater, sugar, and feather-tailed gliders were highly different, each having been shaped in isolation from the other for eons. The genes of these animals are still highly different and yet each of the different hereditary mechanisms guides the development of an analogous result: a nocturnal, arboreal, gliding mammal.

The plasticity of species over evolutionary time that enables unrelated animals to evolve the same lifestyles can be illustrated just as emphatically with Australian birds as with Australian mammals. Biologists have long recognized that most of the songbird groups of Australia, like the Australian marsupials, have evolved in isolation from the rest of the world for millions of years, so distinctive are they in appearance and internal anatomy. But attempts to understand the evolutionary relationships among the Australian birds have been frustrated in the past by uncertainty about whether structural similarities were due to shared ancestry or to independent convergence on a trait adaptive for a shared environmental pressure, like the gliding membranes of sugar gliders and flying squirrels. In 1985, however, Charles Sibley and Jon Ahlquist at Yale University used the same technique they employed to compare the DNAs of ratites and modern birds to examine the evolutionary relationships among the songbirds of Australia. The technique is called DNA-DNA hybridization. DNA is a double-stranded molecule that carries genetic information in most organisms. The two strands are held together because of the bonds between certain components of each strand called bases. The base adenine (A) bonds with thymine (T) only; guanine (G) forms chemical bonds with cytosine (C) only. The attraction between the hundreds of thousands of base pairs in DNA carefully extracted from the tissues of a bird can be overcome by heating the molecule to the boiling point. Then the strands disassociate. If one permits the solution to cool, the DNA molecule will become double-stranded again as the two components pair up in the regions where their base sequences match (e.g., A-A-T-G-T-A on one strand will bond with T-T-A-C-A-T on another disassociated strand).

The way in which Sibley and Ahlquist measured the similarity in the genetic material of two species required that they take disassociated DNA from two species and mix it together at a reasonably high temperature, usually fifty degrees centigrade. Under these conditions the strands will bond together in places (i.e., hybridize) *if* they share suitably long stretches of matching bases. The DNA of species that have evolved recently from a common ancestor will still be fairly similar and will have matching stretches; a large percentage of their DNAs will form hybrids. Species that have a long history of separate evolution will have undergone many genetic changes over time and their DNAs will not hybridize to a great extent.

The numerous technical details associated with this method are somewhat intimidating, but Sibley and Ahlquist have convinced many taxonomists that the system yields precise information about how long pairs of species have been separated. If they are right, their results show that a large proportion of the distinctively Australian songbirds evolved from a common ancestor about sixty million years ago, just before the crustal plate supporting Australia broke away from Antarctica. From this common ancestor arose lyrebirds and bowerbirds (which are especially similar genetically), honeyeaters, logrunners, fairy wrens, fantails, drongos, currawongs and many, many more. This one bird was the starting point for a spectacular radiation of species that look and behave like North American nuthatches, warblers, tree creepers, wrens, flycatchers, and thrushes, to name some of the ecological equivalents of the Australian bird fauna.

Some people like to speculate on what living things would look like on another planet, as if it is necessary to go to Mars to test whether there is a general pattern to life. A trip to Australia is all that is really needed, and it is a lot closer and considerably more hospitable than Mars. Australia offers a natural experiment, a continent isolated from others, stocked with a few odd pioneers, and left alone for fifty million years. Speciation and natural selection produced a grand Australian zoo of marsupials and birds with a catalogue of adaptations familiar to those of us who live elsewhere. There are only so many ways to make a living and only so many good ways to do certain tasks. The good ways have been reinvented by natural selection again and again. That is one of the messages from the Leadbeater's possum, and it is a more sprightly and convincing message when delivered by a living possum bounding along a mountain ash than it would be from a museum specimen, a footnote in the list of species that humans have hurried into extinction.

The Tree of Diversity

A sandy track made by tractors and four-wheel-drive vehicles headed for an isolated fishing beach twists and turns through sand dunes carpeted with an assortment of scrubby plants, few more than a yard high. A handful of twisted trees gains some protection from the wind by crouching in the lee of a stabilized sand ridge rooted to one spot in its old age.

In a shallow basin filled waist-high with prickly shrubs, one plant species stands out, a grand banksia. Although in nearby coastal woodlands *Banksia grandis* reaches a height of fifteen yards or more, here under the constraints of wind and poor soils it is a little shrub. But *grandis* still applies because of its large and striking inflorescences, which are tall, perfect cylinders containing as many as six thousand flowers packed together in close array. The mature inflorescence is a yellow spike a foot high with droplets of nectar at the surface of the woody central axis from which the flowers densely project. To reach the nectar a pollinator must push between the pollen-bearing structures, acquiring pollen in the process that the animal may then transport to another inflorescence on a neighboring plant.

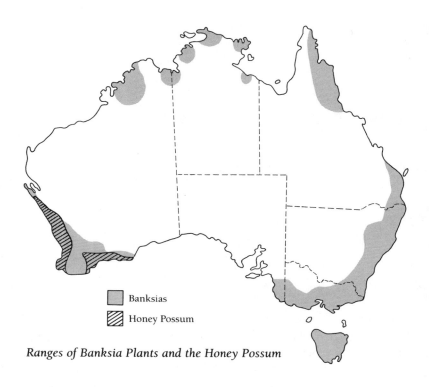

Ranges of Banksia Plants and the Honey Possum

As I walk from one banksia to the next, I occasionally hear rustling as if some small creature were scuttling among the stiff, dry banksia leaves. But it is some time before I finally see a mouselike animal, yellow brown with a prehensile tail and a Pinocchio nose, clinging to the side of a yellow Christmas candle inflorescence. The "mouse" is a tiny marsupial, the honey possum, and it pushes its exaggerated snout through the thicket of flowers to reach the banksia's rich supply of nectar. When it sees me, the possum drops from the flower spike and rackets off through the tough leathery foliage of the plant.

As a *Banksia grandis* inflorescence matures, it turns from yellow to tan to brown; dried flowers begin to break away in tufts, eventually exposing a structure vaguely like a pine cone. If the honey possums, honeyeaters, and native bees have done their work successfully, fat seed follicles bulge out here and there from the surface of the cone. Much later, perhaps under the influence of a fire, the seed cases will burst, ejecting the seeds within to the ground below, leaving behind rows of open mouths calling from the emptied "cone." In at least some banksias, the seeds may contain special reserves of phosphorus that the adult plants have slowly sequestered from the soils on which they grew. Banksias and their relatives thrive on phosphorus-deficient soils, that is, soils that will not support adequate growth of the crop plants that humans value so highly. Because these soils are widespread in Australia, there has been ample opportunity for banksias to spread and speciate, and they have done so with impressive results for persons who value natural variety.

Thus the banksias, like the marvelous array of Australian birds and the smaller but equally delightful set of arboreal gliders, offer another example of the effects of an adaptive radiation of species. The banksia trees whose elaborate flowering parts are jealously guarded by wild-eyed honeyeaters at Pearl Beach and the banksia shrubs probed by honey possums in southwestern Australia are only two of seventy-three species placed in the genus *Banksia*. Although this genus is restricted to Australia, its relatives in the family Proteaceae occur in Africa and South America.

The Africa-Australia-South America connection occurs not just in the Proteaceae but in a host of other plant and animal groups as well, creating distinctive distributional patterns that support the modern (plate tectonics) version of the continental drift hypothesis. Most, if not all, geologists favor the view that at one time Australia, Antarctica, South America, and Africa were a single continent—Gondwanaland. About 135 million years ago the movement of the separate geologic plates underlying Gondwanaland led to the breakup of this continent and the gradual drifting of the various modern continents toward their current positions many thousands of miles apart.

Sometime between fifty and sixty million years ago, Australia achieved independence from what was left of Gondwanaland when it detached from Antarctica. The narrow band of ocean that separated them steadily grew as Australia drifted to its present spot on the globe. The best guess is that around forty to fifty million years ago a member of the Proteaceae in the now isolated Australian continent gave rise to something that could be classified as a *Banksia*. Since that event a great deal has happened within the genus. To appreciate the diversity of banksias most easily it is best to go to Western Australia, where within a day's drive of Perth one can find dozens of species, many of which coexist in the wind-sheared, coastal heath habitat. On a trip to Western Australia after the sabbatical visit this book describes I ranged back and forth along the heaths of the southern coast and encountered a full spectrum of banksias and caught glimpses of the honey possums.

On first glance the heath seems drab and grey beside the brilliant blue ocean that clubs the rocky coast. However, the sweep of tussocky grasses and herbs and the pockets of woodland conceal botanical gems galore, orchids whose overelaborate flowers seem far too substantial for the thin green stalks that support them, insect-eating pitcher plants nearly identical in appearance to those in Minnesota bogs and yet utterly distinct in ancestry and belonging to a separate family altogether, predatory sundews whose pincushion hairdos glow with droplets of glue designed to trap small flies and wasps that descend to sip at the "fluid," and fringed lilies whose magenta flower petals are artfully frayed on their outer edges.

Among the trees that try to maintain a foothold on the heath is *Banksia ilicifolia*, a grey-barked tree with tough serrated leaves and bony limbs. Unexceptional in appearance, *B. ilicifolia* is an exceptionally interesting species because of its *simple* inflorescence. Unlike *B. grandis* and almost all other banksias, the flowers of *B. ilicifolia* are not borne on long central axes but instead emerge from small woody bases. It seems likely, therefore, that the original "*Banksia*" was something like *B. ilicifolia*, at least in the "primitive" construction of its flowers, and that from a fairly ordinary proto-Banksia of this sort has come the explosion of species whose inflorescences are so dramatic, large, and involved that a nonbotanist has to look twice to see

A long-nosed honey possum on its food source, a flowering spike of Banksia grandis.

the connection between the flowery devices of the "advanced" banksias and the homologous structures of *B. ilicifolia*.

And what an explosion, what an aesthetic variety of forms the banksia radiation has produced. On the heath are other tree banksias superficially similar in form to *B. ilicifolia* but with the elaborate inflorescences of *B. grandis* and other species in the main group of banksias. In addition, there are large shrubby species with a celebration of flower spikes that (depending on the species) are deep yellow, or salmon, or yellow-green, held upright like thick candles, Texan in their dimensions, or like colorful artichokes ringed with a set of spiky holly leaves. Other banksias, like *B. nutans*, look like miniature pine trees even to the point of having dangling, chunky, brown inflorescences that resemble pine cones after a fashion. Finally, and strangest of all to a North American, are the prostrate banksias that send their branches creeping *underground* just beneath the surface of the soil; the leathery leaves and beautiful inflorescences of these species poke up through the sand signaling a largely hidden tree beneath the ground. By placing their flowers on the ground these species may encourage small mammalian pollinators less agile than the honey possum to collect their nectar and distribute their pollen. There are five species of these banksias alone in Western Australia, some restricted to a tiny patch of native bush surrounded by encircling wheatfields that have replaced so much of the botanical variety that once grew in the southwestern corner of Australia.

The existing diversity of banksias is an after-the-fact demonstration of the potential for biological variety that existed in the first proto-banksia. Who would have guessed it? Had a biologist existed fifty million years ago, he or she could not possibly have imagined that a relatively simple flowering structure would give rise to the marvelously complex inflorescences of *B. grandis* and others, and that a species of tree or shrub might eventually be the foundation for species of subterranean crawlers. The argument that past form acts as a constraint on the evolution of species is a popular one in evolutionary circles these days. And, of course, the argument has some truth because there is no evolutionary "force" that creates new species from whole cloth. Instead, existing populations are transformed by the processes of selection and chance; new mutations are incorporated only if their altered genetic information is compatible enough with previously existing genes to permit the development of a functional organism. Thus, it seems likely that most changes that are not eliminated at once will be small modifications of the then-typical form.

Although geologists tell us that fifty million years is not such an impressive figure, biologically speaking it is a long, long time. The banksias are testimony to the effect of a gradual accumulation of small changes provided there is sufficient time. No one alteration need be large to reshape a species dramatically if there are thousands of generations for many, many little alterations to create a new population. So to those who speak as if an organism's current developmental plan handcuffs the evolution of novelty, I say, "Tell it to the banksias."

Speaking of novelty, the banksias might point to the long-nosed honey possums scampering about on their flower spikes. The protrusible tongue of this mouse-sized marsupial is even more remarkable than its elongate snout. Not only is the tongue exceptionally long for an animal of its size, but it is blanketed with fine hairs, the better to sponge up banksia nectar, which it transfers into its tubelike, nearly toothless mouth. Furthermore, the honey possum boasts the biggest spermatozoon of any mammal and the smallest neonates (5 milligrams, or 1/2000 as heavy as the mother that produced them) of all the mammals. The testes constitute 4 percent of the male's body weight, an extraordinary figure when compared with the 0.08 percent of body weight for human males. So strange is this animal that it has been placed in a family, the Tarsepidae, all its own. Yet it is obviously a marsupial, for it shares the distinctive reproductive physiology and anatomy of this group. Sometime after banksias evolved, the ancestor of the honey possum became a nectar-feeding specialist, one of the very few nearly exclusive nectarivores among the mammals. The fact that honey possums are restricted to the southwestern corner of Western

Australia probably relates to the exceptional diversity of bank-sias and other Proteaceae there, a diversity that means in every month of the year there are always some nectar-producing species in flower. The selective regime associated with a diet of banksia nectar and pollen is so different from that of the ances-tral group of marsupials from which the original honey pos-sums came that the phylogenetic tracks connecting current honey possums to their ancestors have been obscured. All in less than forty million years. Some experts see a relationship with the macropodid marsupials (the various kangaroos) in such things as the fact that the young are maintained in a well-developed pouch until they reach an advanced stage of devel-opment and that the embryos may be held in a state of arrested development for some time. But one worker who has studied the similarity in the albumin proteins of various marsupials discovered that the honey possum's albumin molecule is re-markably close to that of the petaurids, a group that contains the sugar glider. In the face of this contradictory evidence, no one is ready to claim with certainty who the honey possum's ancestor was.

Now should we be more impressed with the key shared at-tributes of honey possums and their fellow marsupials that en-able us to say with confidence that the honey possum and the koala and Tasmanian wolf had at some point far in the past a common ancestor? Or should we place greater emphasis on the distinctive blood chemistry, chromosome number, immense spermatozoa, and unique diet that label the honey possum a highly specialized species with a long history of its own? Hap-pily, there is no reason to have to make a choice between the two. Each set of features has a lesson for us, one on the conser-vative aspect of evolutionary change that helps us trace histori-cal pathways to some extent, the other on the flamboyant, exuberant creativity of evolution that produces novelties to sur-prise, amuse, and instruct us.

Weaving Their Way Through History

The Green Weaver Ants of Queensland

After the tranquility of the platypus stream in Eungella, we return to the frantic coastal highway of Queensland that rushes in and out of resort towns filled with hotels, beach apartments, fast-food restaurants, fish-and-chips shops, people and more people. The tourist extravaganza eases a bit here and there, and where the real-estate operators have yet to operate there are still forests that run down to the sea. Beneath the dominating eucalyptus, little grass trees stand like unkempt sentinels, conferring their distinctive character on the woodland, just as tree ferns create a special world within a world in the cool, temperate forests of south coastal Australia.

I suspect that Dr. Seuss dreamed up grass trees. They are wildly unlikely plants with absurd tufts of long, grasslike leaves that arch out from the tops of skinny little trunks four to eight feet high. From the unruly topknot of greenery sprouts a thin stalk covered with thousands of tiny white flowers. The plant looks vaguely like a yucca in flower in my own southwestern United States. By elevating its photosynthetic equipment above

139

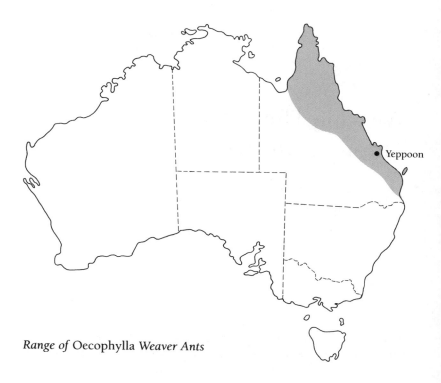

Yeppoon

Range of Oecophylla *Weaver Ants*

the leaf litter, grass trees sometimes save their leaves from ground fires that scamper through the coastal forests near Yeppoon during the hot, dry summers. The trunks of tall grass trees are generally blackened by old burns, providing inspiration for their cheerfully racist nickname, "black boys."

An echidna ambles indifferently among the small, dark-barked eucalyptus, poking its long chocolate nose into loose bark flakes and leaves on the ground. With its tiny eyes and body armor of sharp brown and yellow spikes, the echidna is as improbable as the nearby grass trees.

Overhead a brahminy kite wheels in elegant loops, a hawkish ambassador down from the tropics. It is dressed in an exotically beautiful uniform of rich red chestnut, with a white head and deep brown belly. It sails out over the still sea, helping shape a world of perfection in its passage.

In the trees by the trail, *Oecophylla* weaver ants have constructed their nests from bundles of living leaves tied together with silken threads. Pale green ants walk over the softball-sized nests, ready at a moment's notice to sound an alarm that draws ants by the dozens from within the nest to the surface, where they move about on stiff legs, pointing their abdomens menacingly to a sky patrolled by kites and sea eagles.

Australian green weaver ants are cooperators extraordinaire. Worker ants, both larval and adult, labor together to construct the leaf nests in which they live in their large arboreal territories. To build a nest, hundreds of adults pull in unison to bring two leaves together, sometimes forming rows of living chains that tug a distant leaf into place. This work requires a capacity for integrated group activity that is rarely paralleled in the insect world—or the world of vertebrates, for that matter.

When the edges of two leaves have been drawn close, other workers gather larvae from already-established nests. Each adult holds one white grub in its jaws, with the head of the larva projecting forward. When the worker has maneuvered the grub into the right position, it uses complex communication signals to induce the larva to adopt a rigid pose and to release silk from large internal glands. A silken thread is extruded from a central nozzle on the larva's head, and the adult worker moves the rigid grub back and forth across the gap between the two leaves, weaving a sheet of silk that helps bind the foliage together.

The process is repeated many times over by a great many adult workers and their larval charges to create a suitable enclosure of leaves and stems in which a new brood generated by the queen can be reared and communally defended. The ability to build new leaf homes at will enables weaver ant colonies to expand greatly; as many as 500,000 individuals may occupy and defend a territory that embraces several whole trees over which the ants range in search of their insect prey.

We can with good reason wonder how such an "advanced" (complicated) business could have ever evolved in the ants. Bert Hölldobler and Edward O. Wilson were puzzled by the high-tech weavers, and in order to satisfy their curiosity they collected the evidence needed to construct a plausible historical sequence leading to the amazing weaver societies of *Oecophylla* ants. They were able to decipher the track of history, thanks to the existence of other ants with less complex, more "primitive" forms of cooperation and weaving. These other species are not direct ancestors of *Oecophylla* weavers, but their existence shows what kinds of ant societies can evolve and therefore provides clues as to what the actual ancestors of weaver ants may have been able to do.

We can begin to trace the historical steps to the "advanced" weaver ants by asking how it is that larval weaver ants came to possess such massive silk glands, which develop when the larvae are only half-grown. There are a great many ants in which larvae have silk glands, but these appear only in the final larval stage just prior to pupation, and they are used not to weave nests but to form a protective silken cocoon in which the ant turns from grub to adult. Because cocoon-weaving is so widespread among the various groups of ant species, it seems likely that the trait originated in a very ancient ancestral species of ants, including *Oecophylla* weavers. The ancestor of weaver ants almost surely produced larvae that developed silk glands just prior to pupation, using the manufactured silk solely to build themselves useful cocoon cases.

However, silk glands once evolved can be used for other purposes, such as building a protective nest. The larvae of one genus of arboreal Brazilian ants do indeed contribute a bit of silk that helps reinforce a nest composed largely of chewed vegetable fibers. The role that silk plays in nest-building is modest in these species, and the larvae often add silk to the nest when unattended by an adult worker. When they are held in the jaws of a nestmate, the larvae move back and forth, using movements similar in form to those that they will employ when making a cocoon. In contrast, larval *Oecophylla* weavers never release silk unless an adult signals them to do so, and they keep their bodies immobile, letting the adult worker move them back and forth.

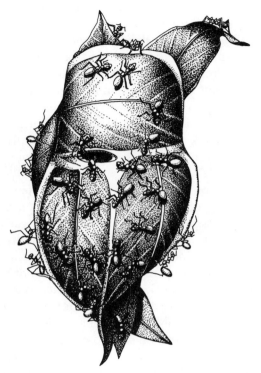

A nest of the green weaver ant with agitated workers on its surface.

The point is that if complex weaving was originally derived from cocoon-building, something like the behavior of the Brazilian arboreal ants offers a plausible first step in a sequence that leads to *Oecophylla* societies. The changes in behavior required for the first step, the incorporation of silk in a nest, are simple. Once a "primitive" degree of weaving had been established in an ancestor of *Oecophylla*, it could have been further modified by additional moderate changes to reach a stage intermediate between the most rudimentary form of nest-weaving and the supersophisticated methods employed by green weaver ants in Australia.

Something like the intermediate stage may be represented by

living ants of several genera, one of which builds nests of silk and litter fragments, surrounded by leaves that are tied tightly together with additional silk. This yields a more complex woven nest than that of the Brazilian tree ants, but, like those ants, the larvae produce silk only in their last developmental stage and they, not their adult handlers, perform the weaving movements. On the other hand, like *Oecophylla* the larvae of these ants no longer actually build cocoons but pupate naked. Nor do they add silk to the nest unless specifically stimulated to do so by a worker that carries them to the spot where silk is required.

From this sort of intermediate stage only a few more small modifications are needed to achieve the silken mastery of Australian weaver ants. Because they produce silk earlier in their larval life, there is more of it available to build nests, and through the cooperation of workers in manipulating leaves, the sites available for nesting are expanded. We do not need to propose that the exceptional skills of *Oecophylla* weavers arose in a single stroke. Instead we can see how these wonderfully adept creatures could have evolved through a gradual series of slight behavioral and developmental shifts associated with small alterations in the habitats taken as nesting sites. The fabric of evolution is a cloth woven thread by thread, each new change adding to and building upon what has been established in the past.

Life with Others

The evolution of society fits the Darwinian paradigm in its most individualistic form. Nothing in it cries out to be otherwise explained. The economy of nature is competitive from beginning to end. Understand that economy, and how it works, and the underlying reasons for social phenomena are manifest. They are the means by which one organism gains some advantage to the detriment of another.

Michael T. Ghiselin

Fairy Penguins

Running a Gauntlet Together

A roaring winter wind churns the waters in Bass Strait just off Phillip Island. Flocks of starlings dart out from the island and cut into the gale, swirling and dipping over the water to an islet a short distance offshore. There they settle onto a great sloping hillside, sheltered against the cold, only to lift up again like an oversized blanket blown away from the grasses in the dimming light of late afternoon.

We leave the starlings to battle the wind, and we drive to the large parking area by the penguin reserve. There is room for hundreds of vehicles, for the reserve is a popular tourist spectacle, seen by more than four hundred thousand people annually. Most visitors make the short trip down from Melbourne in an afternoon. On this bitter day only a few dozen cars have parked; the tourists straggle through the tufted sand dunes to assemble on a concrete-tiered observation deck overlooking Summerland Beach. Massive breakers roll into the U-shaped cove while people watch the wind-buffeted ocean and wait patiently.

Port Phillip
Penguin Reserve

Range of the Fairy Penguin

In the twilight a guide begins to talk through a loudspeaker, telling us a little about the natural history of penguins and urging parents to keep a rein on their children. Chasing penguins is not permitted, and flash photos are out, too.

Soon the penguin's caretaker turns on a number of floodlights that illuminate a small section of the beach, where waves spill great foamy surges of water far up the smooth sand. In the spotlit area the first penguin pokes its head from a beach-thrown wave but then drops down to be carried out to sea again.

Shortly, small groups of fairy penguins assemble where the isolated bird had been. The birds are social, although their "societies" are simple and temporary, unlike the complex, long-term communities of green weaver ants. A pod of penguins stands in the surge, having been swept inland as far as possible. These are tiny penguins only about a foot high, but penguins unmistakably, blue-grey-backed and white-fronted. They wait uncertainly, looking about, as the water rises and falls about them. One bird panics and dashes back into the breakers; the others immediately flop into the surf and are swept into the ocean.

Eventually, however, some more resolute birds wash up onto the beach, stand their ground, and then walk with penguin dignity out onto bare sand to the delight of the temporary society of humans gathered to watch them. The little birds gather momentum as they cross the twenty to thirty yards of open beach that separate them from the sand dunes. Once into the grassy dunes, they promenade along depressed trails created by thousands of penguin feet over the centuries. They pad solemnly inland, dispersing along private side-trails that lead to their sleeping burrows where they will spend the night until returning, before dawn, to the sea.

Penguins arrive sporadically in the wild surf over the next thirty to forty-five minutes. Their human audience dwindles as the novelty of fairy penguins fades. The guide turns off the spotlights and instructs those who remain to return to their cars. Soon the fierce wind reclaims the beach.

My colleague at Monash University, Mike Cullen, and I have permission to stay, but most of the birds have come ashore, as the caretaker had predicted, except for three small, ghostly penguins that march up the concrete ramp on which we sit, swaying past in a bowlegged sailor's gait under the winter's pale moon.

The Phillip Island crowd that watches fairy penguins each night ought to be both charmed and puzzled by their behavior. Why do they put on this show for us? Why do they come ashore at all, particularly during the nonbreeding season when there are no chicks to feed in nest burrows?

Although it might be possible for the penguins to spend the night floating at sea, there could be two disadvantages for individuals that did so. Night-hunting sharks or other marine predators that can track their prey by scent could find a sleeping penguin adrift among the waves and eat it, demolishing its opportunities for future reproduction. Moreover, the fairy penguin, although well-insulated by its coat of feathers, is a small animal with a correspondingly large surface-to-volume ratio. Water extracts heat from an animal twenty-five times more effectively than air of the same temperature. At air and water temperatures likely to affect penguins off southern Australia, individuals in the water are forced to raise their metabolic rate from twenty to 100 percent compared to birds on land. By moving ashore and into inland burrows on an island with no large mammalian predators (because they have not been able to swim to the island), a fairy penguin might gain protection from marine enemies and an improved environment for heat retention.

The nightly return to land does, however, create one serious problem for the penguins. A penguin among the dunes does not move with the grace of Rudolf Nureyev, nor can it dive beneath the soil's surface if threatened from above. Large hawks and eagles patrol island beaches for carrion and vulnerable living prey, and a fairy penguin offers an exotic but tasty meal for a white-breasted sea eagle, or a large raven, or a massively billed Pacific gull.

Fairy penguins appear to have countered these threats in several ways. They come to their island burrows only in the evening, when visually hunting predators cannot see well and have often retired to roosts of their own. Moreover, the penguins move up the beach only in the company of many companions. The adaptive value of sociality under these conditions can be illustrated with the following example. Imagine that there is a deadly predator lurking on the beach that will capture, kill, and eat one penguin sometime during each evening. If a penguin is in a group of five when the attack takes place, it has a 20-percent chance of departing this world, but if it does not run the gauntlet until a company of twenty-five birds has assembled, it will improve its odds of survival fivefold. This is the dilution effect, the survival advantage an animal gains simply by being social, by being a part of a group of prey to dilute the chance of being the unlucky victim selected by an enemy. If the dilution effect does apply to fairy penguins, we can understand the extreme reluctance of the first penguin to leave the wave surge and venture up the beach alone and isolated.

The dilution effect has been invoked to account for such diverse phenomena as the immense winter roosts of millions of monarch butterflies at certain places in California and Mexico and the formation of large nighttime choruses of certain tropical frogs. Both the butterflies and the frogs have predators that

A pod of the world's smallest penguin, Australia's fairy penguin, in the surf on Phillip Island.

attack with great efficiency—grosbeaks that pluck chilled monarchs from their perches and bats that snatch calling male frogs from the water with great, raking hind feet. A few dedicated biologists have counted the deaths occurring in large and small groups of these animals, and there is no doubt that a member of a large group has a higher probability of living to see another day than one attached to a smaller group. Under these circumstances it is easy to see how a great fondness for the company of others might evolve. For fairy penguins in the water, looking out for number one is the impetus for the development of a rudimentary society, a society whose members care nothing for each other, but are simply playing a numbers game and "hoping" their number doesn't come up.

A Society of Muttonbirds

To reach Port Campbell National Park to the west of Melbourne, I must first navigate for an hour and a half across the city. Captain Cook felt no greater sense of relief upon securing his passage through the shoals of the Great Barrier Reef than I do upon weaving through the tumult of left-handed city traffic to reach the relative safety of the highways beyond.

The boats of Port Campbell rise and fall in the small and barely protected harbor, a notch in the huge yellow sea cliffs that run for miles along the coast here. Winds off a cold ocean have sheared the heathlands smooth. Here and there a stick of a tree twists and bends in a futile attempt to escape the force of the southerlies. Enormous breakers roll forward, pushed by the wind, to assault the massive barrier that confronts them. Waves erupt against rock, sending explosions of white sea spume into the air. Despite the apparent stability of the cliffs, the waves are winning, gradually consuming the land. Because the rock erodes unevenly, great stacks of stone remain scattered and abandoned in the blue-and-white ocean, surrounded by water,

Range of the Short-Tailed Shearwater,
or Muttonbird

untoppled for the moment but marking the gradual victory of
the sea.

Some of the vertical stacks have flat upper surfaces covered
by an acre or so of stunted heath, and these serve as nesting
sites for the short-tailed shearwater. The shearwater gets its
common name of "muttonbird" because the nestlings bulge
with stored fat, and Australians have collected them for oil and
food from colonial times to the present.

Muttonbird Island is cut off from the mainland by a narrow
channel that waves have carved in recent geologic time. A side
road from the coastal highway runs down to the ocean cliff near
the stack and ends in a little car park on a tiny exposed promontory. From this point one can supposedly see the shearwaters. But the adult birds can be watched only in the evening,

when after a day spent at sea they return to dig their burrows in the ground or, later, to feed the single fat chick within their burrows.

Today, at the start of the breeding season, I wonder if the birds will appear on cue. A hard gale blows in from the southwest and the faint sun intermittently casts an unwholesome yellow-grey light on a steely ocean. A fine mist from waves broken on the cliff face swirls up two hundred feet, coating the windshield with a grimy salt film. The campervan rocks in the wind; on the radio a German poet discusses his epic work on the sinking of the *Titanic*.

A short distance from Muttonbird Island a deep and narrow trench digs into the cliffs. In the midst of a fierce winter storm in 1878, the *Loch Ard*, a magnificent clipper ship bound for Melbourne from London, ran aground on a reef about a half mile offshore. The ship's master had failed to see the Otway Light and had come too close to land. The *Loch Ard* quickly began to break apart, and the fifty-two people on board desperately launched lifeboats into the wind, fog, and blackness of the terrible sea. To see the surf erupting against the cliffs in daylight is proof that there could have been no hope for lifeboats headed toward that coast at night in even a moderate gale.

Two people miraculously survived, a sailor who was blown under an overturned lifeboat into the narrow inlet, now called Loch Ard Gorge, and a young woman clinging to a ship's spar who also slipped into the gorge. The woman did not reach the tiny sandy beach at the end of the cleft but was trapped against the cliff. The sailor heard her cries, and in the night he reentered the freezing water, overcame the battering waves, and rescued her.

On the radio the German poet explains that the *Titanic*'s fate is a metaphor for the destiny of modern society. I scan the ocean fruitlessly for shearwaters. Once a great white gannet cuts over the waves, riding the wind with swaggering ease on huge, black-tipped wings.

As dusk inches across the apparently lifeless ocean, a small black mote appears, so minute and so far away that it may only be a product of wishful thinking. But it is a shearwater. And soon a line of the birds materializes, then another, as if through spontaneous generation. The shearwaters cruise the ocean, tacking back and forth on sharp wings that almost touch the stormy surface of the sea as they carry the birds slowly toward the cliffs.

As evening arrives, shearwaters reach the stack and begin to rise far above the ocean in their approach to land. A few birds race with the wind and loop over the mainland before sailing back to Muttonbird Island. They strafe the island on black wings before fluttering down to disappear into the green heath.

An adult muttonbird sitting at the entrance of its nest burrow.

The wind continues its relentless attack. In the deepening evening, arriving shearwaters slide through the greyness, barely visible in the mist and the day's slow decay.

The short-tailed shearwaters that swirled over Muttonbird Island on that stormy evening were the survivors of an extraordinary migration that is repeated every year by millions of adult birds. After the summer breeding season ends in April or May (autumn in the southern hemisphere), the shearwaters move to New Zealand's Tasman Sea and then go north across the equator to the northwestern corner of the Pacific Ocean. Later, in anticipation of a new breeding season, the birds permit westerlies to carry them across the Pacific and down along the west coast of North America. From there they swing back across the equatorial Pacific and over to eastern Australia, arriving at a multitude of muttonbird islands in September to renew the cycle.

The advantages to individuals of participating in such an extravagant migration, twenty thousand miles of traveling as a shearwater flies, must lie in the ability of migrant birds to feed both in southern and northern oceans at times when these waters are richest in marine life, while avoiding terrible winter storms. Shearwaters pay a large price to secure these benefits, for in some years vast numbers return to Australia so weakened by the long flight home that they perish without breeding, and their bodies wash up on Australian beaches amid the sea wrack.

At times on their migrations and during the breeding season, the birds are highly social, traveling in dense flocks of thousands, skimming over the waves, a few stiff wingbeats, then a long glide, a few more wingbeats, another long glide. Social life in fairy penguins appears to have evolved in response to the threat of predation. Could the same factor be responsible for the flocking behavior of short-tailed shearwaters? If the predation hypothesis is correct, there should be at least some observations of predators attacking shearwaters. The only predators that threaten migrating shearwaters might be the Pacific gull, white-breasted sea eagle, or peregrine falcon. But these hunters operate close to shore, and if their actions over evolutionary time have favored shearwaters that clumped together to dilute the risk per individual of being killed in an attack, the tendency to flock should be greatest close to shore. The discovery of great flocks far out at sea would weaken the predation hypothesis (unless we also discovered special predators at work in pelagic environments).

But we must also consider alternative hypotheses for flocking that do not invoke predation. Perhaps individuals that group together can confuse and capture their prey more efficiently than isolated birds. Or perhaps one shearwater improves its flight efficiency by closely following another, if air that has passed over the lead bird's wings provides a more aerodynamic environment than unmodified turbulent air. (Long-distance migrants, such as Canada geese, that travel together in V-formation can in theory fly 70 percent farther than a solo bird with the same energy expenditure because of drag reduction associated with the V-flight pattern.)

Although the list of possible explanations for flocking in shearwaters could be expanded, we have looked at a sufficient number to demonstrate that hypotheses abound. What little evidence exists to help us discriminate among these ideas supports the predation hypothesis to some extent. The parallels with the unrelated fairy penguins are numerous. Like the penguins, shearwaters gather in the late afternoon near their burrows but do not approach shore until dusk has arrived. At times they can be seen floating on the water in great rafts, or simply drifting back and forth over the ocean, so the delay in landing has nothing to do with the necessity to hunt for food during every possible daylight hour. Instead it looks as if individuals wait until a great armada of shearwaters has assembled and until partial darkness impairs the vision of waiting gulls, hawks, and eagles before the shearwaters come ashore to the safety of their island burrows. Moreover, the *Complete Book of Australian Birds* claims that short-tailed shearwaters do not raft in places where predators are absent; if this could be carefully documented, it would provide extremely powerful support for the predation hypothesis as an explanation for flocking near the coast.

In light as dim as light can be, I strain to catch a last glimpse of a late-arriving muttonbird. The surf thunders against the coast. I am glad to be in the campervan and not on the *Titanic* or the *Loch Ard* just before they went down, when I would have had a chance to study the nature of social behavior in humans more closely than I desire.

Flying Fox Mothers
Know Best

In the course of our family travels we once more fill every cranny of the campervan with clothes and celery, wine and sleeping bags, and drive off in search of a new temporary home. Our route takes us north along the coast of New South Wales and then west into the interior. We stop for the night at Dorrigo.

From the van, where we lie in early morning grayness, we can hear birdlike twitters and chitterings produced by a vast but distant congregation of mysterious creatures. I speculate that we are listening to a roost of English sparrows, but this proposal stimulates justified skepticism. When we get up we find that the caravan park selected late last night borders a forest grove of great buttressed trees filled with thousands of fruit bats. They grip the upper branches of the giant trees with hooked feet. Hanging upside down, wrapped in their black membranous wings, they look like huge, rotting, black-skinned fruits.

Range of the Grey-Headed Flying Fox

The glade echoes with their incessant bickerings, birdlike but harsh and querulous. Here and there individuals drop head-first from their perches to avoid a snappish neighbor and seek a more congenial resting site elsewhere. They sail through the air on measured wingbeats; with a wingspan of four feet and long, sharp, reddish faces, it is easy to see why they are called flying foxes.

As the sun warms the dangling bats in the treetops, one animal extends a wing and begins to wave it slowly back and forth, like a matron with a fan in her church pew on a summer Sunday.

Flying foxes are a living demonstration of the interaction of feeding ecology and predator pressure in shaping an animal's social behavior. The several species of flying foxes and the other members of the large and diverse family of fruit bats rely heavily on fruits for their daily bread. Actually, most consume fruit juice primarily, for they rarely consume the pulp or seeds but instead use their jaws as cider presses, sucking down the fluid while expressing the solid remainder, which dribbles to the earth below. Flying foxes are not fastidious about what fruits they will consume, feasting on whatever is readily available, whether it be domesticated plums or mangoes. Their enthusiasm for orchard-grown produce has made them more than mildly unpopular with orchard owners.

Under natural conditions the most abundant Australian flying fox would have supported itself by eating fruits of native figs supplemented with nectar lapped from the sweet flowers of eucalyptus. When fig trees set fruit or eucalyptus come into bloom, they generally produce a profusion of resources. The abundant food provided by tropical fruiting and flowering trees offers the foundation for dense populations of flying foxes. Because individual trees provide food for relatively short periods and at long intervals, the bats do not take up residence in a particular tree or small area. Flying foxes are big and mobile; they get up and go long distances in search of bonanza trees. Thus instead of dispersing throughout the forest, large numbers of bats gather together in semipermanent "camps," no doubt strategically located to enable foragers to monitor a large, profitable region.

By forming camps, some of which contain fifty thousand bats, the camp's members may enjoy some of the advantages derived from diluting the impact of predators, advantages similar to those enjoyed by social fairy penguins. Fruit bats do have a veritable rogue's gallery of enemies, including pythons, eagles, goannas, and crocodiles, although how crocodiles manage to grab fruit bats on the fly is a mystery to me. The flying fox's large size helps protect it against many other potential predators, and indeed only the very largest species of bats gather together in conspicuous, open-air roosts. Most other bats hide during the day in caves, under leaves, behind bark, or even in warthog burrows, where one intrepid Canadian researcher searched for and found a rare African bat he was after.

Although flying fox camps appear chaotic, they have a social organization. In trying to understand the structure of flying fox societies, the Australian researcher John Nelson was handicapped by the lack of a large number of clearly marked individuals, although he was able to recognize certain bats by the pattern of bullet holes in their wings, mementoes of a close call with an armed Australian fruit farmer.

Despite a shortage of marked bats, Nelson gradually deduced that females tend to cluster in small portions of the roost and that males compete directly for control of harems, employing the female-defense strategy of male resin wasps and lions. Much of the jabbering and aggression so obvious in a big fruit-bat roost occurs as males struggle for possession of small territories, a yard or so of limb, from which hang one or more desirable females. Males announce their ownership of a branch section by rubbing it with secretions from a shoulder gland. If a male is successful in maintaining possession of a site, he may eventually mate with the females that use the limb as their habitual hanging place.

Once inseminated, females undergo a six-month gestation period, terminating in the birth of a single large baby who weighs almost half as much as its mother. At first, females cart this heavy luggage around when they fly off for fruit snacks, but after a week or so they leave the burdensome progeny behind, suspended from a limb in the camp. Potential problems arise when a mother flying fox returns to nurse her offspring, for the youngsters frequently move about in dense clusters of juveniles, all of which appear identical to human observers. Several young bats may importune a returning female in an attempt to get some milk from someone other than their mothers.

Similar "milk-thievery" has been observed in other highly colonial bats, such as the Mexican free-tailed bat. This insectivorous species gathers by the millions in suitable caves in the American Southwest. Lactating females return to masses of babies left clinging thickly to cave roofs and are aggressively pursued by hosts of milk-hungry infants. For fruit bats and

A flying fox sailing before a giant rainforest tree, which has many other fruit bats dangling from its branches.

free-tailed bats alike, the question is, Who should receive a mother's milk?

An evolutionary biologist would predict that females should feed only their biological offspring, for only by nurturing her baby is a female likely to propagate her distinctive genes (of which half are carried by her infant). But the first biologists to study Mexican free-tailed bats were convinced that this was impossible in the confusion of the cave nurseries and that females therefore picked pups at random to receive their milk. These batmen argued that with up to forty aggressive free-tailed bat pups jumbled together on a patch of cave roof no larger than a small floor tile, a female coming back from a nighttime feeding trip could hardly be expected to find her infant within the crèche in total darkness.

But despite sound reasons for thinking that the task is impossible, free-tailed bat mothers do *not* dispense their milk randomly after all. Bat researcher Gary McCracken employed a sophisticated technique that involved taking blood samples from females and the young they were nursing to show that females offer parental services to their own offspring around 80 percent of the time.

Fruit bat mothers are every bit as selective when it comes to serving up milk; females deal very brusquely with begging babies other than their own. Nelson believed that a female could recognize her own pride and joy by its specific odor and distinctive vocalizations—subtle cues, to say the least, for human bat watchers, but sufficient for female flying foxes, thanks to the millions of years of natural selection that have favored females that bestowed their maternal benefits strictly on their own pups.

The power of selection for parent-offspring recognition in colonial species whose mothers run the risk of aiding someone else's progeny can be seen in the many cases of convergent evolution of this ability. Not only have the distantly related Mexican free-tailed bats and Australian flying foxes evolved the capacity to recognize their own young, so too have many other social animals. For example, bank swallows, like many bats, breed in dense groups. Semi-independent young wander about within the colony, begging for food from individuals other than their parents. Food-laden adult swallows are set upon by foreign fledglings, but despite the risk of misdirecting their parental care, the adult swallows are remarkably skillful at rejecting thieves and giving their catches to their own offspring. Moreover, the recognition system is similar, for adult swallows learn to identify their babies by their distinctive vocalizations, each individual producing its own vocal signature. In this way, bank swallows "selfishly" direct most or all of their reproductive effort to promote their own genetic success, just as predicted by biologists using the adaptationist approach.

The existence of juvenile food thieves in colonial swallows and bats is just one demonstration that social life has both pluses and minuses. When individuals come together for some mutual advantage, such as improved protection from predators, they also may try to take advantage of each other in various ways. The constant squabbles in a fruit bat colony remind us that "social" is not synonymous for "free from conflict." Animals are only social to the extent that this advances their personal reproductive chances; the recognition of this point has been slow in coming but quick to bear fruit as a guide for what to look for in the lives of social animals from bank swallows to flying foxes.

Bell Miners, Lerps,
and Kinship

Busloads of schoolchildren out from Melbourne run up and down paths among the animal enclosures set in an open forest at the Sir Colin MacKenzie Reserve at Healesville. The elongate leaves of eucalyptus gums point downward, absorbing the sunshine, ornamenting the woodland with colors running the gamut from pale blues and powdery whites to somber greens. The kangaroos in their grassy pens endure the stares of visitors. A male red kangaroo takes his ease, hind legs sprawled across the lawn, head raised, like a bather on a beach inspecting the passing crowd and daydreaming the time away.

A rufous fantail in pursuit of an insect flits out of a willow near the ibis rookery. Its orange-red tail flares behind it like a parachute. With a twisting dive the bird finds a landing spot on a limb along which it scampers with erratic and mechanical movements. From a dead stub over its head, a white ibis barks indelicately.

The brilliant "tink-tink" of the bell miners rings through a stand of mature gums. The miners sound as though they

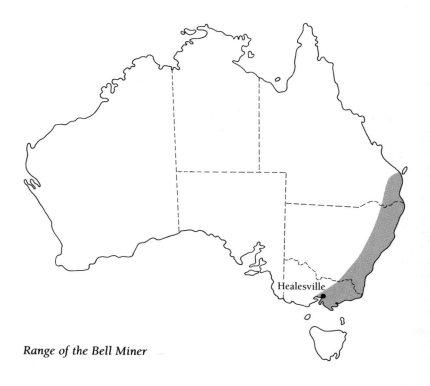

Range of the Bell Miner

are everywhere, but they reveal themselves only occasionally. Decked out in warm, yellow-green plumage, they cling to the thin outer twigs of a eucalyptus like plump, ripening fruits.

Bell miners are members of that quintessential Australian family of birds, the honeyeaters. Most species in the family, like the New Holland honeyeater we met earlier, possess slightly down-turned, long, thin bills that they use to probe for nectar in the flowers of banksias, grevilleas, and eucalypti. Bell miners, however, are endowed with relatively short bills, not particularly well suited to extract food from the deep-throated corollas of nectar-containing flowers. Appropriately enough, bell miners feed not on nectar but instead on a group of plant-sucking bugs called psyllids. These true bugs often reach infestation levels in patches of eucalyptus forest, where they suck sugary sap from trees at such a rate that they can weaken or even kill their hosts. Bell miners eat the young bugs (or nymphs) and the sugary coverings (or lerps) that the nymphs secrete to protect themselves from ants. So bell miners actually do drink "nectar" of a sort, but only after it has been processed through the guts of insects.

One might imagine that, because bell miners destroy nymphal psyllids, eucalyptus would benefit from their presence. But Australians have noted that wherever the birds occur (and bell miners live in conspicuously noisy colonies containing dozens of individuals), the trees look unhealthy for as long as the birds are there (and a colony may persist for forty years). Thus bell miners either lack the ability to reduce populations of psyllids, or they actually help maintain the infestation in some way.

In order to identify the nature of the relationship between psyllids and bell miners, a group of Australian researchers removed all thirty-four birds from a forest stand under heavy attack by psyllids. They captured the bell miners in fine nylon nets and released them far away in another psyllid-infested woods. The exiled bell miners did not return, nor was their old stomping grounds taken over by a new colony of the species. Within four months, the psyllids had been eaten into extinction.

The agents of eradication consisted primarily of smaller birds, such as sitellas, pardelotes, thornbills, and treecreepers, that moved into the woodland immediately after the bell miners had been carried off. By watching these newcomers closely and measuring their feeding rates, the research group estimated that they were gobbling up psyllid nymphs and psyllid lerps at more than twice the rate of the now-departed bell miners. Furthermore, the newcomers downed lerps and nymphs with equal gusto, whereas the honeyeaters often carefully removed just the lerp shield from a nymph's back, leaving the nymph alive, well, and able to produce a new covering in a few days. Because the bell miners' replacements did not husband the psyllids but consumed them as quickly as possible, the insects soon disappeared.

Thornbills and sitellas live much of the year in pairs. A pair can defend a small breeding territory but not a large stand of trees infested with vast quantities of psyllids that attract a host of invaders with a fondness for these tasty insects. Thus it pays the individuals of these less social species to eat the goose that lays the golden lerp; if a pair of sitellas were to try to "farm" a psyllid colony, other birds would simply rustle the prey away.

Bell miners, however, are highly cooperative birds that together can keep thornbills, sitellas, and other bell miners out of a psyllid-infested area. The harsh, churring alarm call of one miner draws its companions to the spot. Together they mob intruders that would eat their psyllids, driving them off and protecting a food supply that they manage for long-term yield rather than for short-term gain.

Here is another advantage for individuals that live together— mutual defense of a territory containing a valuable food that other species would deplete. Bell miners also cooperate in mobbing and distracting their predators, so that by living socially they not only protect their food but themselves and their progeny.

A skeptical adaptationist, however, would want to know how the food supply preserved by a band of bell miners was divided among the members of the cooperative. Do all the birds in a colony get an even cut? Do all birds breed equally? If not, why do nonbreeders help others, if they can reap no reproductive return for their investment in social aid?

Questions of this sort motivated a study by M. F. Clarke, who examined a color-banded population of thirty-seven birds for some years. Clarke found that the group was actually composed of two clans, each of which had its own living space within the study site. When the southern clan was attacked by a group of noisy miners (another species of communal honeyeaters), the northern clan permitted their fellow bell miners to be chased

A bell miner about to swallow an edible lerp it has plucked from the back of a psyllid bug.

out (and probably doomed to death) rather than come to their assistance. Clarke's genealogical records revealed that each clan consisted of a separate collection of relatives. Within each extended family were a few breeders and many nonbreeding individuals that guarded communal territory boundaries, chased off psyllid eaters, brought food for nestlings, and attacked predators.

Nonbreeding helpers-at-the-nest have been found in a substantial number of bird species, but still only a tiny minority of the total number studied. Their existence in any animal raises a fundamental evolutionary problem, for how can the self-sacrificing behavior (or altruism) of nonreproducing helpers survive over time? The occurrence of helpers poses a threat to Darwinian theory, which predicts that there should be no examples of evolved actions that reduce an individual's chances of leaving descendants.

We can begin to work our way out of this corner by recognizing that the evolutionary significance of reproduction stems from the fact that one's offspring carry 50 percent of one's own genes (the genes in the egg or sperm of an individual that reproduces sexually). A helper that assists its parents to produce a brother (or sister) that otherwise would not have existed makes an "offspring equivalent," for siblings also share 50 percent of their genes in common, thanks to having the same parents. Therefore, helping close relatives can be fundamentally the same thing as reproducing personally in terms of its impact on the propagation of the helper's particular genes. Helpers that increase the survival of relatives are actually creating carriers of their hereditary material indirectly rather than through the direct method of personal reproduction. Now we can understand why, in evolutionary terms, members of the northern clan did not risk their lives to defend unrelated members of the southern group, and instead reserved their altruistic tendencies for their fellow clan members, with whom they shared genes.

What at first looks like a possible contradiction of natural-selection theory turns out instead to be a confirmation of its underlying logic, the logic of the adaptationist approach. Only traits that help individuals pass on their genes directly or indirectly are likely to persist in populations over time and be represented in living species. The extended families of bell miners do not know that their behavior constitutes a kind of test of evolutionary rules. They continue unruffled to farm their psyllids, gang up on sitellas and pardelotes, and lunch on lerps.

Adaptive Altruism

I . . . will confine myself to one special difficulty, which at first appeared to me insuperable, and actually fatal to my whole theory [of evolution by natural selection]. I allude to the neuters or sterile females in insect-communities; for these neuters often differ widely in instinct and in structure from both the males and fertile females, and yet, from being sterile, they cannot propagate their kind.

Charles Darwin

Superb Blue Wrens

Calculated Helpers

A yard-long goanna noses through the short grasses in the Wimmera River's floodplain. Its reptilian body is mottled black and grey with a few unwholesome flecks of pink. The spacious parklike woodlands of the Little Desert National Park bask in tranquility until the big lizard spots me. It sprints noisily toward a nearby river red gum and scrabbles up the smooth trunk toward a broken hollow limb parallel to the ground and twenty feet above it. The goanna seems to flow into the opening at the limb's end, a long grey lizard down a deep black hole.

Nearby, the forest gives way to a wet grassy pan, bordered by sand ridges covered with an olive heath. In the pan a few trees stand next to shallow pools of water; dense hummocks of shrubbery rise like giant beehives from a smooth green lawn. A troop of superb blue wrens pops out of one hummock and travels to another while one male sings his complex trilling song from a perch. The singer is a spectacular bird with a radiant cerulean blue cap, cheek patch, and back set against a deep, iridescent, blue-black background. There are several males in

Range of the Superb Blue Wren

adult plumage in the group, as well as a number of females and juveniles, pale brown and long-tailed out of all proportion to their size. The males scamper, flicker, and flit amid the foliage, glowing with blues no other animal can duplicate.

Although superb blue wrens have the same general body form and the same jaunty way of holding the tail cocked high in the air as the North American wrens, they belong to a separate family of birds and have a social system that does not resemble that of the more familiar wrens. The Australian ornithologist Ian Rowley discovered the complex social organization of superb blue wrens by capturing all the birds in an area near Canberra; each captured bird received a set of colored plastic legbands that identified it distinctively thereafter. By plotting the sightings of marked birds over the period from 1956 to 1960 and keeping track of who was breeding with whom and how many offspring they had, Rowley became one of the first to study reproductive cooperation in a bird species.

The wrens sometimes live together in the male-female pairs so typical of birds generally, but they more often form groups of as many as six individuals that communally defend year-round territories in which they forage and breed, much in the manner of bell miners. When a band of three or more wrens occupies a territory, only one male and one female reproduce. The others are supernumeraries, as Rowley called them, or

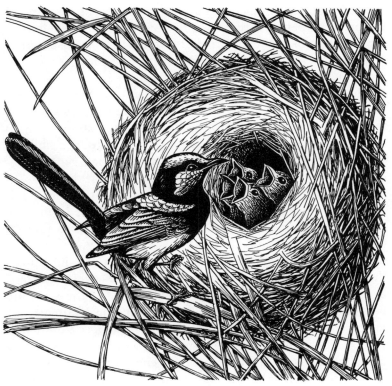

A male superb blue wren at its nest.

"helpers-at-the-nest" that do the same kind of things as their counterparts among bell miner clans. They guard territory boundaries, join in the evening chorus that deters intruders, preen their fellow group members, and most significantly help feed the nestlings and fledglings produced by the breeding pair. This help is particularly handy when parents are able to turn a group of fledglings over to a supernumerary male so that they can immediately return to the business of producing and rearing nestlings. As a result of the assistance of helpers, the annual production of a pair is raised from 1.5 independent offspring (the average for two birds that lack helpers) to 2.8, the average for pairs with one or more supernumerary assistants.

Who are these altruistic helpers? Rowley's patient work showed that supernumeraries are generally recent offspring of the breeding pair that remain with their parents and help care for later broods. Male offspring are particularly predisposed to stay on for a year or more as helpers before leaving to seek their reproductive fortunes elsewhere.

The difference between the sexes in the readiness to sacrifice or postpone a chance at personal reproduction suggests that for males the superior route for passing on genes is more likely to involve a period during which the male helps produce siblings, whereas females are more likely to maximize their genetic success by rearing their own little wrens. Why might this be so?

The key may lie in differences in mortality rates for adult males and females. Perhaps because they do all the incubating and are more vulnerable to nest-assaulting predators as a result, females are killed more often than males. This creates breeding opportunities for surviving females, favoring young individuals that disperse to take advantage of these chances. In contrast, because males usually live longer than females, the sex ratio becomes male-biased. The likelihood of finding an unguarded mate in a suitable territory is therefore reduced for males. Young, unattached males tend to remain with their parents, because for them the indirect route of gene propagation is likely to be more profitable, whereas for females the direct route is more apt to lead to a genetic payoff.

This argument can be subjected to closer scrutiny by taking advantage of the fact that the degree to which males outnumber females varies from year to year. When the sex ratio of a population is close to 1:1, we can predict that males should forget about helping and attempt to reproduce personally, for with equal numbers of females and males there will be more chances for success through personal reproduction. But when the number of males greatly exceeds the number of females helping by males should prevail for reasons just discussed. These predictions have been tested. In two years in which females happened to be reasonably abundant, only about 10 percent of breeding pairs had male helpers. But in a year when females were outnumbered 2:1, about 50 percent of breeding couples had supernumerary sons on hand to help rear the young.

The wonderfully aesthetic superb blue wren is yet another creature, like the New Holland honeyeater, whose members can adjust their behavior to secure maximum genetic advantage under different environmental conditions. It is looking more and more as if "bird brain" is not quite the slur we imagined it to be.

The Sisterhood of
Cerceris Wasps

With the full-fledged arrival of summer we abandon Melbourne and head for Pearl Beach in New South Wales, where the University of Sydney has a biological station superbly located within walking distance of a magnificent sandy crescent beach. Sydney itself lies only a short distance to the south, but between us lies a coastal forest bordering a fantastically irregular seashore cut and carved by rivers and inlets. In our niche by the beach we feel continents away from urban life.

Large lizards roam the lawns of the station under the predatory gaze of the kookaburras; they hunt both lizards and barbecued lambchops, which they pluck in a wild flurry of wings from our picnic plates. During the day we join the Australians on the beach and watch the waves come in and the hours slip away. The shark patrol flies back and forth across the bay.

Up in the forest, the heat desiccates the eucalyptus trees and converts woodland litter to tinder. A pyromaniac has a field day, setting fires that sweep the hillsides with a black broom; volunteer fire fighters go out time and again, controlling one blaze only to be faced with another.

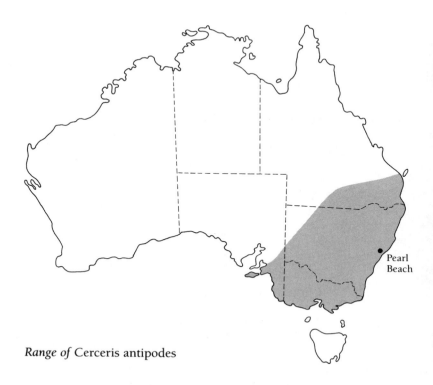

Range of Cerceris antipodes

On orange sandy tracks through the forest, tiny mounds reveal dark entrances to hidden burrows. The piles of freshly excavated sand soon blow away, leaving barely visible holes scattered along road margins. By crouching down one can peer into a slanting tunnel and there at the entrance will be a wasp, a half-inch long, with big eyes and yellow face, holding her ground before the fantastic creature whose shadow obscures the sun.

The road-digging wasp, *Cerceris antipodes,* belongs to a family of solitary digger wasps, the Sphecidae. Typically, wasps in this group burrow into soil and construct a brood cell at the end of the tunnel. They capture prey that they paralyze and carry to the brood cell, where the female lays an egg on an insect destined to be food for her young. After the egg is laid the cell is sealed off and the mother wasp sets about building a new brood cell or a new nest altogether, repeating the cycle until her death. A female digger wasp usually never sees her mature offspring and does all the work of nest construction and prey capture entirely by herself without assistance from any other individual—with the result that sphecid wasps are often called solitary wasps.

Sphecids vary a great deal behaviorally despite having a standard pattern of nesting behavior. For example, consider the matter of nest design. Females of *C. antipodes* dig burrows that may be twenty-five inches long, with many separate brood cells scattered along a main tunnel that descends to eight inches or so beneath the surface. Other wasps construct nests that range from only a couple of inches long to more than a yard long and a yard deep, depending on the species. Incidentally, successful excavation of the more complex nests requires a variety of simple tools, a delicate touch, plenty of time, and good luck.

The preferred prey of solitary wasps also varies by species. *C. antipodes* specializes in small, chrysomelid leaf beetles, whereas other members of the genus *Cerceris* hunt totally different families of beetles. Still other digger wasps take flies, or bees, or caterpillars, even butterflies and damselflies. Wasps commonly carry their paralyzed prey with their middle legs as they zip back to their nests. But there are many alternative transport techniques, one of which involves the use of a special clamp on the tip of the wasp's abdomen that holds the prey while the female flies through the air.

Most intriguing of all, not all solitary wasps are solitary. Although most follow the typical sphecid pattern outlined above, in a few species females do not live apart but share the same burrow. *C. antipodes* is one of the rare communal sphecids. I first realized this when I watched a prey-laden female come sailing in to her nest entrance, embracing a beetle with her legs while holding her victim's antenna in her jaws, only to be "greeted" by another wasp stationed in the nest opening. The wasp at the entrance slipped back quickly to let her colleague plunge into the nest before immediately stepping forward again to use her head to block the burrow once more.

Observations of this sort inspired me to carry out a study of the wasps using Rowley's technique of marking individuals. This was accomplished by netting females as they entered or exited their burrows, removing them carefully from the insect net, and placing a dot of enamel paint on the thorax of each wasp. Because the wasps were so small, they could not sting me and had to endure the temporary humiliation of being handled without making any effective response.

Although my project lasted less than a month, and not five years as Rowley's had, I was still able to learn a great deal about these animals once I had a population of marked females to observe. Two to eight individuals occupied each nest during the month, and as many as four were seen on a single day at some nests, confirming the communal nesting behavior of this sphecid. Usually, however, only one (or at most two) females went out to hunt chrysomelid beetles on any given day. The remainder stayed behind, with one female guarding the opening to the nest tunnel.

The guard wasps remove windblown debris that would otherwise impede beetle-carrying females as they attempted to enter the nest. It is probably important for a provisioning female to get into her burrow as quickly as possible, for prey-laden wasps are plagued by little miltogrammine satellite flies that move behind them as if attached by a string. At the last moment, just as a wasp enters her nest, these flies attempt to place their larvae on the prey item. This requires a degree of athleticism worthy of applause, for the fly must give birth to a small grub and glue it onto a small beetle tightly gripped by a flying wasp in an instant. Any satellite fly that succeeds in doing this harms the wasp because the fly grub will feast on what the wasp's offspring would otherwise have had for itself.

The countering tactic of the wasp is to approach the nest and dive at high speed directly into the shaft of the nest tunnel, without alighting at the entrance, thus making it difficult for a trailing fly to catch up and larviposit at the correct moment. If the entrance were partially blocked by sand or leaf debris, the wasp would have to pause and scrabble her way in, increasing the vulnerability of her brood provisions to the gymnastic fly parasite.

Guard wasps also deal directly with a variety of other parasites that walk over the ground searching for undefended nest entrances. If successful, these parasites slip down into the burrow and make for brood chambers, there to exploit food intended for *Cerceris* grubs. Guards thwart these enemies, for although the wasps are small in size, they are endowed with large curved jaws, which they use to snap at and intimidate parasitic flies and other nest intruders.

A female Cerceris *wasp clutching her beetle prey as she flies to a nest entrance guarded by a female nestmate, probably her sister.*

Among the category of intruders are wandering females of their own species. If we can generalize from what is known of other similar species, guards probably identify individuals by their distinctive scents. Nestmates share an olfactory badge and guard wasps grant these individuals free entry into the nest while repelling those with foreign odors.

Nestmates may share a similar odor because they are relatives. I gathered some evidence on this point by excavating a few burrows, a tedious but revealing task. I found within some nests the remains of many old brood cells in the section of the burrow closest to the entrance. In more recently constructed portions there were new brood cells, some with individuals just about to metamorphose into new adults. This information, in conjunction with similar findings by students of other *Cerceris* species, suggests that nests may be used for more than one year, and that some of the second-generation females may remain to occupy their natal nest, adding extensions to it and sharing living quarters with their relatives. If they can recognize one another through odor cues or other means they can prevent unrelated females from taking advantage of a laboriously dug burrow while permitting members of their family to exploit the benefits of living together.

But do some members of an extended family of *Cerceris* wasps derive more benefits than others? Are some individuals sterile guards, while others collect prey and lay eggs? Records of marked wasps show that females of this species are not locked into one role for life. A guard female may later become a provisioner, and later still revert to guarding the nest. In addition, when I examined the ovaries of a sample of collected females I found that most of the wasps in a nest had fully developed ovaries, with at least one large mature egg. These discoveries make it extremely unlikely that *C. antipodes* has evolved a social system like that of the ants, termites, and certain bees and wasps, in which the division of labor is rigidly defined with only one (or a few) reproducing queens and a host of functionally sterile females that carry out the nonreproductive chores of colony life.

Instead, the social system of *C. antipodes* shares some basic characteristics with that of the superb blue wren. In both species, some members of a group spend a portion of their lives helping their relatives, in the wasp's case by nest-guarding and perhaps by digging new brood cells and tunnel extensions to a nest. During this time they may indirectly propagate some of their genes through the increased reproductive success of the relatives they have assisted; the relatives' offspring carry some of the same genes that are carried in the bodies of the helpers. But when good opportunities for personal reproduction arise, the wren and wasp helpers can take full advantage. When a breeding male wren dies, one of his sons will promptly switch from supernumerary to reproducer, inheriting the territory of his father and his father's mate, which may be his mother or a stepmother. Likewise, the ovarian status of *Cerceris* females strongly suggests that they can lay eggs whenever the situation permits, thereby passing on genes directly as well as indirectly.

I would like to know, however, the precise nature of the interactions within a communal burrow of *Cerceris* wasps. Do provisioning females always lay eggs in the brood cells they personally fill? If two or more females are provisioning simultaneously, do they work in separate brood chambers? Do nest guards or others try to oviposit in cells that a hardworking nestmate has provisioned? Are some females prevented from egglaying by their sisters? If so, do such females leave home to seek their reproductive fortunes elsewhere? The answers to these and many other questions about the lives of *Cerceris* wasps remain well hidden in their underground tunnels. I suppose there is no special urgency to the search for the answers to these questions. But once you have watched the trim little wasp at work on perfect summer days near a perfect Australian beach, you develop a special affection for them and want to know all there is to know about their lives.

A Happy Family of
Grey-Crowned Babblers

Mount Isa in western Queensland reminds me of my home state
of Arizona, for it is a mining town dominated by a huge smoke-
stack like any number of mining communities in the southwestern United States. Kites and other hawks circle over the
center of Mount Isa, drifting in and out of a plume of pollutants
from the stack. I stop long enough to restock my groceries and
have a repair shop replace the battered shocks on the campervan. Then, having done my bit to stimulate the local economy,
I explore the surrounding low red hills.

The late afternoon sun illuminates the bone-white trunks of
ghost gums, which rise from the pale grasses like skeletons
breathed to life by an aboriginal shaman. On an austere hillside, massive termite mounds, eight feet high and constructed
of a pale grey material as hard as cement, shoulder the scattered
gums to one side. The great mounds project the melancholy air
of Easter Island monuments. Clumps of spinifex clothe the
rugged slopes with thin green needles, each a foot or two in

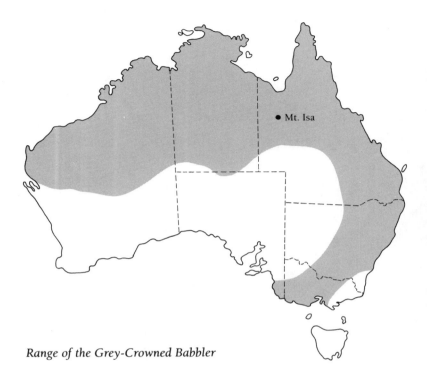

Range of the Grey-Crowned Babbler

length. A pair of red-brown spinifex birds emerges from the center of a spiny patch. They climb the thin seed-bearing stalks to which they cling like marooned marsh wrens far from water.

A group of grey-crowned babblers travels a low line of trees that sketches the course of a dry creek bed. The babblers fill the air with cheerful conversation, oblivious to the descending sun. Brown and grey with broad white eyebrows, they look like plump thrashers. But they fly with none of the furious wing-flapping of thrashers, preferring to drift along on spread wings from perch to perch, probing and poking with long curved bills for insects in foliage or under bark on the ground.

One babbler sounds an alarm; its harsh "chaks" send the band scuttling for cover into a tangled thicket of greenery that has retained its color despite the dryness of winter. Silent ghost gums monitor the stillness that remains after the birds' retreat.

Grey-crowned babblers are yet another of Australia's communally breeding birds. With social behavior like that of the superb blue wren, they live in family groups of three to twelve birds; the parents reproduce and their sons and daughters form a band of helpers that defend the groups' domain, protect the nest, and feed nestlings and fledglings. They travel everywhere together and even sleep communally in "dormitory nests," masses of twigs scattered about a territory, so that they have a choice of where to spend the night. Their highly social nature is reflected in one of the common names bestowed upon them—"happy family."

The number of babblers in a social unit varies considerably, and this variation provides a way to analyze a nagging problem in studies of helpers-at-the-nest: Do helpers really help? Rowley's blue wren study showed that groups with helpers fledged more young than groups without them, but results from various other studies have been more ambiguous. In many cases, researchers have been unable to find clear-cut evidence of increased reproductive success due to helpers, and several biologists have suggested that helpers may actually interfere with the activities of a breeding pair in order to secure breeding rights of their own eventually within the group territory.

To resolve this problem for one species, American ornithologist Jerram Brown and his coworkers first measured fledging success in large-versus-small groups of grey-crowned babblers. They found, as had Rowley with blue wrens, that the parents' reproductive success was positively correlated with the number of individuals in a group. But they pointed out that the correlation does not unequivocally prove that the extra birds are the reason for the elevated reproductive success of the breeding pair. Perhaps pairs that secure a good territory have many offspring that live to become "moochers," but the parents continue to have many fledglings because their territories are resource rich, not because of the supernumerary offspring that continue to live at home after fledging.

To control for the possible effects of territory quality on reproductive success, Brown devised an experiment in which he first located twenty bands of babblers with six to eight members each. From nine of the groups he removed all but one of the nonbreeding birds, leaving the breeders with a single potential assistant; the other eleven groups were left intact with their three to five nonbreeding cohorts. If territory quality had enabled all twenty bands to reach a relatively large size and to produce many offspring per breeding bout, removal of most of the nonbreeders should have little effect on the reproductive success of a babbler pair. Indeed, by eliminating some of the moochers in a territory, there might be more food for the parents and their nestlings, thereby increasing the production of fledglings.

As it turned out, the groups with fewer supernumeraries fledged on average only 0.8 young, whereas intact bands with more helpers had significantly more, 2.4 on average. This experimental result strongly supports the hypothesis that, in grey-crowned babblers at least, helpers really help. This is not to deny that, in other species living in different environments, "helpers" may be in it to manipulate others in attempts to reproduce personally. Nor is it unlikely that conflict will arise among babbler helpers over matters of succession when one of the breeding members of the group dies. Nevertheless, the presence of helper babblers has an overall positive effect on the reproductive success of a breeding pair. And this is to the genetic advantage of the helpers, for by rearing extra brothers and sisters, which share half their genes on average, they pass on their genetic material by proxy, increasing the representation of their genes in future generations. The time they spend waiting to become breeders is not wasted but is used to further a genetic goal.

A cluster of cooperating babblers seems entirely different from a wary, contentious knot of silver gulls waiting for a campground handout. And yet individuals of both species be-

A grey-crowned babbler at a communal nest.

have in ways that tend to proliferate their bits of DNA, their units of heredity. Knowing this, we can begin to make sense of their distinctive actions, understanding that the unrelated gulls in a mob attracted to a rich food source are each competing to monopolize as much food as possible, whereas the cooperation that exists among a happy family of babblers arises because of their shared genetic heritage and shared ultimate goals.

The babblers need not know why they tolerate, perhaps even like, the company of other members of their family. It is enough that their brains, shaped by eons of natural selection, induce these birds to behave in the best interests of their genes. The band continues along the wash, which even without water holds a powerful attraction for them. I listen as warm whistles, yahoos, and babbler chaks fill the empty spaces among the ghost gums and dying grasses.

Nasute Termites

Sterility Is a Fertile Topic

About halfway between outback Queensland and the tourist-dominated seacoast, Carnarvon Gorge cuts deeply through a dry prairie, covered in early autumn by tall yellow grasses and black-barked gum trees. Mobs of pretty-faced wallabies sprint from the borders of the dirt track, whose dust-filled potholes and iron-ridged corrugations threaten to shake the campervan to pieces before we ever reach our destination.

Once the descent into the gorge is complete, a whole new universe appears abruptly, like a magician's show-stopping illusion. A stream has inched its way through the limestone prairie, excavating a canyon bit by bit. The stream sustains a richly varied subtropical forest along its border within the gorge. Giant palms and huge eucalyptus rise greenly against the tan cliffs. Tame kangaroos, campground lagabouts, hop forward solemnly in search of a handout, while crowlike currawongs perch on our van and fix us with their penetrating yellow eyes.

Along the boulder-cluttered stream there are cycads growing beneath taller trees, looking like trunkless palms whose tops

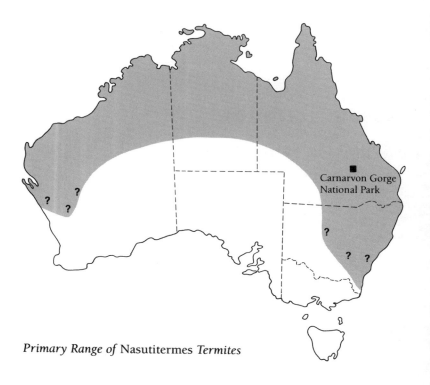

Primary Range of Nasutitermes *Termites*

have been thrust into the soil. Poisonous red fruits gleam from the center of the plants' crowns.

In the middle of the creek an azure kingfisher perches on a boulder that breaks the slow flow of the water. The tiny bird is adorned with magnificent blue feathers on its head and back that contrast with the rufous belly and pert red face. It points to the water with its long black bill.

A small trail leads away from the main stream to enter a side canyon and climb up a steep and sandy slope atumble with fallen blocks of grey stone. A yellow cliff stops further progress, creating a long, smooth, sheltered overhang whose walls are a gallery of carvings and paintings—a legacy of generations of now-extinct aborigines. The paintings were fashioned by aboriginal men who filled their mouths with a reddish liquid ocher and then forcefully sprayed the paint over a hand or boomerang, a method that leaves behind a stenciled image when the sprayed object is removed. In the warm light of midday, emu footprints made by spray painting the tips of boomerangs march implausibly but beautifully straight up the rock wall. Scarlet honeycreepers forage in the trees below us, flickering like flames among the pale green leaves.

Near the trail, a thin red-brown tube runs up the massive trunk of a dead eucalyptus. I make a small opening in the fragile tunnel, exposing pale termites within. The small-jawed workers recoil from light and hurry into darkness; in their place appear the larger, browner soldiers with their great pointed noses. I send a puff of air toward them, and in quick response the dark-headed soldiers shoot out tiny silver threads of glue which hang in the air for a moment, attached to their noses.

Nasute termites get their name from the large noselike extensions of the bulbous heads of their soldiers. Within a soldier termite's head a set of powerful muscles surrounds a very large gland filled with a liquid that becomes sticky upon contact with the air. Soldier termites, alerted by alarm scents released by workers near a breech in the tube, will confront any ants that invade their home. Even though the soldiers are totally blind, they are able to locate an intruder by touch or by the air movements an enemy creates. Pointing their noses at the invader, they fire, entangling it in a Lilliputian web of sticky silken strands. This disables intruders, keeping them from doing much damage to the workers that serve a queen and king, which live deep within an underground bunker connected to the foraging tubes.

The evolution of the extraordinary societies of termites, of which the many nasute species are but one subgroup, is one of the great puzzles in biology. Termite colonies may contain millions of individuals, most of which belong to one of several possible castes, each with its specialized functions, every member integrated into its greater society, thanks to the sophisticated communication system of the species.

From an adaptationist perspective, the most remarkable feature of a termite society is the permanent sterility of its vast army of workers and soldiers. Unlike blue wren or babbler helpers, which are quick to reproduce if social conditions permit it, a soldier termite is totally committed to altruism and the indirect route of genetic propagation. Nothing like absolute sterility has evolved in any vertebrate, except perhaps in the naked mole rat, which like termites lives underground in groups and forages for food from within tunnels laboriously constructed by teams of workers in the cementlike soil of African plains. Both naked mole rats and termites live in extended family groups, and most individuals are sterile workers whose activities assist parental reproduction. From time to time the reproducing animals may produce reproductive offspring that leave their natal colony to form a new one elsewhere. However, the extent to which workers in naked mole rate families are obligated to a lifetime of sterility, like worker termites, is uncertain at the moment.

There are other insects whose societal organization is similar to that of the termites, even to the point of having a specialized soldier caste to defend workers and parents against all enemies at all costs. These insects, which include the ants and certain species of bees and wasps, belong to the order Hymenoptera, and are not closely related to termites, which have an order of their own, the Isoptera. Thus complex sociality has evolved independently among the insects several times, just as helpers-at-the-nest have arisen in any number of distinct families of birds.

The life-history pattern of all social insects is marked by the deferred production of reproducing offspring by the founders of a colony. A queen termite or ant first lays eggs that become worker offspring that do not themselves reproduce but instead devote all their lives to helping their parents. Eventually the

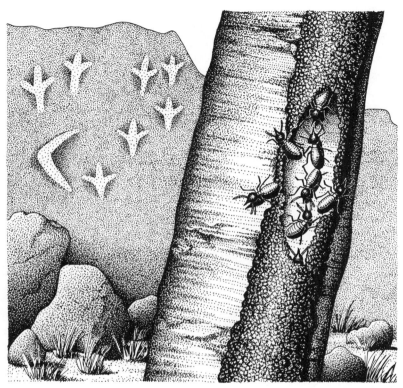

Nasute termites at a breach in a covered foraging tube running up a dead tree trunk.

queen of a social insect colony begins to generate offspring that can disperse and reproduce. The striking cost of this system from the standpoint of the queen and king termites is the chance that they will be discovered and killed by an enemy before they ever have a brood of reproducing offspring. If their family consists only of workers and soldiers when they are dispatched, their genes will die with them with no opportunity to be passed on to the next generation. But if a pair of termites lives long enough and has a helpful worker-soldier force in place, these sterile assistants will enable them to produce re-productive offspring in great abundance. Perhaps the great in-crease in productivity at this stage is large enough on average to compensate the king and queen for the risks they take to reach this point.

This argument must remain largely speculative in the ab-sence of data that could address some important questions. First, what is the probability that a pair of termites of a given species will reach the phase when effective reproduction can begin? Second, do sterile nurses, soldiers, and foragers create a sufficient number of reproducing brothers and sisters to com-pensate them for their reproductive self-sacrifice? Even if these data were available, we would still want to know what it is about the environmental pressures facing termites, the social Hymenoptera, and perhaps the naked mole rats, too, that make deferred reproduction a better tactic for a king and queen than immediate efforts to manufacture reproducing offspring.

Termite tubes are like aboriginal pictographs, the graffiti of a largely unknown society, rich in hidden meaning, symbolic of how much more we have to learn about ourselves and the animals that share our world.

Rock Wallabies on the Road to Birdsville

From the dusty caravan park in Normanton, where brown apostle birds float from tree to fenceline like a cloud of animated leaves, I travel south toward my last destination, the road to Birdsville. My stay in Australia has nearly run its course. Already my family has returned to the States, and soon the short-tailed shearwaters and I will cross paths, the birds headed over the Pacific Ocean toward the southern coast of Australia while I fly far above them in the opposite direction.

But there is still time for a short trip, time for a drive down the road toward Birdsville. The town, hundreds of miles away, is perhaps the most famous pure-outback hamlet in central Australia. As best as I can judge from photographs of the place, the heart (and most of the body) of Birdsville is a tiny single-story hotel, from which beer can be purchased, perched beside an incongruously broad dirt road on the edge of the Simpson Desert.

Traveling outside Mount Isa, the car, which had been operating smoothly, suddenly skips a beat; little sparks of fear jab

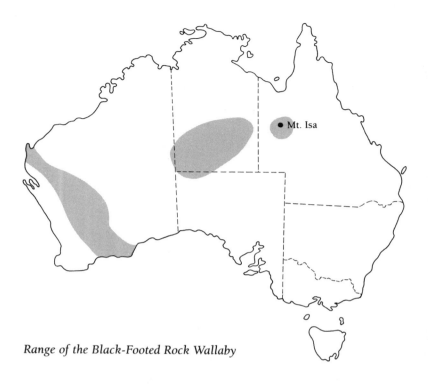

Range of the Black-Footed Rock Wallaby

upward in my chest. The engine does it again. And again. I stop along the deserted road, miles from a mechanic. I go through the motions, opening the metal flap so that I can inspect the engine, which I do with the assurance of a chimpanzee peering at an advanced treatise on metallurgy. After poking here and there I shut the engine cover with resignation. It strikes me that although the campervan has had any number of mechanical problems during our brief relationship, every one has been different. I have never learned a thing from a past difficulty that has served me in dealing with a current trouble.

But miracles do sometimes occur. The engine starts cleanly, the car strikes out again confidently, roaring along as if it were fresh out of a repair shop. I am bewildered, but I know enough to be grateful.

As we move forward, I begin to listen less and less for new signs of engine failure and turn my attention to my surroundings. Ahead of me and not far off in the grasses I can see the head of a bustard. This is a welcome surprise. I had not expected to see the bird, which is said to be increasingly rare. I stop to look. The bird ignores me and strolls calmly through prairie grasses that reach its shoulder. Bustards are huge birds, as big as turkeys but more sleek and athletic in appearance. The Australian species' sandy brown plumage nicely matches the color of the Queensland winter plains. Bustards walk with their beaks held up at a slight angle, which gives them a faintly supercilious air, as if they were looking down their noses at their fellow creatures, so many of which are smaller than they.

As I study the bustard with my binoculars, a pickup truck stops fifty yards down the road. The two men in the truck also appear to be looking at the bustard with interest. Suddenly I have the disconcerting sensation that I am back in Arizona, where every other pickup truck has a gun rack, for I see that one of the men has a rifle. Their interest in the bustard does not stem from an enthusiasm for ornithology. It is illegal to shoot the bird, but the species is reported to be highly edible, one of the reasons why its populations are on the wane. I decide to wait the hunters out, for they may be reluctant to blast the bird in front of a witness. After a bit the armed man pulls his door shut and the truck guns past, leaving the bustard to stalk its grasslands awhile longer.

There is a hint of desert in the yellow plains, a measure of openness and the suggestion of surprises. But despite the lure of the road I do not get anywhere near Birdsville. In fact, the few miles that I travel in its direction are all on the sealed portion of the highway. I do not have the time, and even if I did, I would be nervous to venture far from Mount Isa because I have come to view the van the way one does a well-meaning but accident-prone friend. And rightly so, for unknown to me she already has a slight crack in her engine block that will substantially reduce her value on the used-campervan market.

But it feels right to make a gesture in the direction of the

Rock wallabies on a great jumble of boulders that is their home in western Queensland.

untamed outback. The narrow strip of pavement unwinds to the south and I follow, discovering an area with great jumbled stacks of sandstone boulders that provide dramatic relief from the flatness of interior Queensland. The stacks resemble African kopjes, and I almost expect to see lions reclining on their smooth ledges. When I climb among the rocks I can look for miles across the earthy Queensland veldt decorated with other rocky outcrops and the omnipresent eucalyptus, the local species tall and broad-crowned like African acacias on the Serengeti Plain.

The animals that call these kopjes home force me to acknowledge that for the moment I am in Australia and nowhere else. Rock wallabies live here, and in some of the mountainous piles of boulders a dozen or so animals stand on their kangaroo feet at vantage points all round the outcrop, like lookouts on a castle under siege. As I approach them, the delicate little kangaroos exhibit amazing grace, leaping confidently from one rock to the next, across chasms, up steep inclines, in one acrobatic maneuver after another. What is the history of this species? Are they descended from a plains-dwelling ancestor something like the modern red kangaroo? How has life among the rock piles shaped the structure and behavior of the wallaby? Is each kopje occupied by an extended family group? Do they cooperate more than mobs of unrelated individuals, like the pods of fairy penguins on a Port Phillip beach, drawn to one another to dilute the risk of capture by dingoes or some now-extinct predator?

I soon retrace my route, leaving the wallabies and my unanswered questions behind. Passing slowly again through a tiny roadside hamlet, I cross a low bridge over a dry wash. In the gravel streambed seven aborigines sit crosslegged in a circle round a wine jug. A black hand waves, beckoning me to join them. Is the man friendly, or drunk? Is his wave really an invitation, or a sardonic send-off to a stranger? I am tempted to stop but afraid to take the chance, and so carry on, missing a chance to learn firsthand about aboriginal attitudes toward kookaburras and their songs.

Later that day in my solitary campsite far to the east of the kopjes and the aboriginal drinking party, I hear the hooting of kookaburras. Kookaburras live in communal clans that proclaim dominion over a territory by singing together at dusk as well as at dawn, following the same pattern used by superb blue wrens. Their maniacal calls reverberate through the woodland. I am glad to have kookaburras with me at the end of my journey. They are amusing, noisy company, a symbol of Australian animals, a source of questions worth considering.

Suggested Reading

Two important general works on Australian animals and natural history are the *Reader's Digest Complete Book of Australian Birds,* published in 1976 by the Reader's Digest Service Pty. of Sydney, and *Australia, A Natural History,* by Howard and Mary Alice Evans, published in 1984 by the Smithsonian Institution Press of Washington, D.C.

Below I have listed key articles and books that provided information on the animals whose behavior I have discussed in the chapters of this book.

Selection and the Silver Gull

Galusha, J. G., and J. F. Stout. 1977. Aggressive communication by *Larus glaucescens. Behavior* 62:222–235.

Tinbergen, N. 1953. *The Herring Gull's World.* London: Collins.

Red-Tailed Black Cockatoos Meet Dr. Pangloss

Gould, S. J., and R. Lewontin. 1979. The spandrels of San Marco and the Panglossian paradigm: A critique of the adaptationist programme. *Proceedings of the Royal Society of London (B)* 205: 581–598.

New Holland Honeyeaters and Adaptive Math

Paton, D. C. 1982. The diet of the New Holland honeyeater *Phylidonyris novaehollandiae. Australian Journal of Ecology* 7:279–298.

Paton, D. C. 1984. Food supply, population structure, and behavior of New Holland honeyeaters *Phylidonyris novaehollandiae* in woodland near Horsham, Victoria. In *Birds of the Eucalypt Forests and Woodlands: Ecology, Conservation and Management*, J. A. Keast, H. F. Recher, and H. A. Ford (eds.). Canberra: Australian National University Press.

The Unromantic Duet of Northern Logrunners

Sonnenschein, E., and H.-U. Reyer. 1983. Mate-guarding and other functions of antiphonal duets in the slate-colored boubou (*Lanarius funebris*). *Zeitschrift für Tierpsychologie* 63:112–140.

Paternal Paragons Among the Mallee Fowl

Frith, H. 1956. Temperature regulation in the nesting mounds of the mallee fowl, *Leipoa ocellata* Gould. *Commonwealth Scientific and Industrial Research Organization Wildlife Research* 1:79–95.

Frith, H. 1959. Breeding of the mallee fowl *Leipoa ocellata* Gould. *Commonwealth Scientific and Industrial Research Organization Wildlife Research* 4:31–60.

Cupboard Love and Thynnine Wasps

Alcock, J. 1981. Seduction on the wing. *Natural History* 90 (Dec.): 36–41.

Mate Choice by Female Hangingflies

Thornhill, R. 1983. Cryptic female choice and its implications in the scorpionfly *Harpobittacus nigriceps. American Naturalist* 122: 765–788.

Spotted Bowerbirds

Borgia, G. 1985. Bower destruction and sexual competition in the satin bowerbird (*Ptilonorhynchus violaceus*). *Behavioral Ecology and Sociobiology* 18:91–100.

Borgia, G. 1986. Sexual selection in bowerbirds. *Scientific American* 254 (June): 92–100.

Pruett-Jones, M., and S. Pruett-Jones. 1983. The bowerbird's labor of love. *Natural History* 92 (Sept.): 48–55.

Singing in the Rain

Lill, A. 1979. Nest inattentiveness and its influence on the development of the young in the superb lyrebird. *Condor* 81:225–231.

Lill, A. 1980. Reproductive success and nest predation in the superb lyrebird *Menura superba*. *Australian Wildlife Research* 7: 271–280.

Resin Wasps and

Water Wasps Down by the Waterhole

Smith, A. P., and J. Alcock. 1980. A comparative study of the mating systems of Australian eumenid wasps (Hymenoptera). *Zeitschrift für Tierpsychologie* 53:41–60.

Thornhill, R., and J. Alcock. 1983. *The Evolution of Insect Mating Systems*. Cambridge, Massachusetts: Harvard University Press.

Cassowaries

McGowan, C. 1984. Evolutionary relationships of ratites and carinates: Evidence from ontogeny of the tarsus. *Nature* 307:733–735.

Stapel, S. O., J. A. M. Leunissien, M. Versteeg, J. Wattel, and W. W. de Jong. 1984. Ratites as oldest offshoot—Evidence from α-crystalline A sequences. *Nature* 311:257–259.

The Bad Rap on Marsupials

Low, B. S. 1978. Environmental uncertainty and the parental strategies of marsupials and placentals. *American Naturalist* 112: 197–213.

Duck-Billed Platypus

Griffiths, M. 1978. *The Biology of the Monotremes*. New York: Academic Press.

A Once and Future Possum?

Sibley, C. G., and J. E. Ahlquist. 1985. The phylogeny and classification of the Australo-Papuan passerine birds. *The Emu* 85:1–14.

Henry, S. R., and G. C. Suckling. 1984. A review of the ecology of the sugar glider. In *Possums and Gliders*, A. P. Smith and I. D. Howe (eds.). Sydney: Australian Mammal Society.

The Tree of Diversity

George, A. S. 1985. *The Banksia Book*. Sydney: Kangaroo Press.

Johnson, L. A. S., and B. G. Briggs. 1981. Three old southern families—Myrtaceae, Proteaceae and Restionaceae. In *Ecological Biogeography of Australia*, vol. 1, A. Keast (ed.). The Hague: Dr. W. Junk bv Publishers.

Renfree, M. B., E. M. Russell, and R. D. Wooler. 1984. Reproduction and life history of the honey possum, *Tarsipes rostratus*. In *Possums and Gliders*, A. P. Smith and I. D. Howe (eds.). Sydney: Australian Mammal Society.

Weaving Their Way Through History

Hölldobler, B., and E. O. Wilson. 1983. The evolution of communal nest-weaving ants. *American Scientist* 71:490–499.

Fairy Penguins

Stahel, D. C., and S. C. Nichol. 1982. Temperature regulation in the little penguin, *Eudyptula minor*, in air and water. *Journal of Comparative Physiology B* 148:93–100.

A Society of Muttonbirds

Lissaman, P. S., and C. A. Schollenberger. 1970. Formation flights of birds. *Science* 168:1003–1005.

Serventy, D. L., V. Serventy, and J. Warham. 1971. *The Handbook of Australian Seabirds*. Sydney: A. H. and A. W. Reed.

Flying Fox Mothers Know Best

McCracken, G. F. 1984. Communal nursing in Mexican free-tailed bat maternity colonies. *Science* 223:1090–1092.

Nelson, J. E. 1965. Behavior of Australian Pteropodidae (Megachiroptera). *Animal Behavior* 13:544–557.

Bell Miners, Lerps, and Kinship

Loyn, R. H., R. G. Runnals, G. Y. Forward, and J. Tyre. 1983. Territorial bell miners and other birds affect populations of insect prey. *Science* 221:1411–1413.

Superb Blue Wrens

Emlen, S. T. 1984. Cooperative breeding in birds and mammals. In *Behavioral Ecology, An Evolutionary Approach*, J. R. Krebs and N. B. Davies (eds.). Sunderland, Massachusetts: Sinauer Associates.
Rowley, I. 1965. The life history of the superb blue wren *Malurus cyaneus. The Emu* 64:251–297.

The Sisterhood of Cerceris Wasps

Alcock, J. 1980. Communal nesting in an Australian solitary wasp, *Cerceris antipodes* Smith (Hymenoptera, Sphecidae). *Journal of the Australian Entomological Society* 19:223–228.

A Happy Family of Grey-Crowned Babblers

Brown, J. L., E. R. Brown, S. D. Brown, and D. D. Dow. 1982. Helpers: Effects of experimental removal on reproductive success. *Science* 215:421–422.

Nasute Termites

Eisner, T., I. Kriston, and G. J. Aneshansley. 1976. Defensive behavior of a termite (*Nasutitermes exitososus*). *Behavioral Ecology and Sociobiology* 1:83–125.
Wilson, E. O. 1971. *The Insect Societies*. Cambridge, Massachusetts: Harvard University Press.

Index